INEQUALITY

WHAT EVERYONE NEEDS TO KNOW®

INEQUALITY

WHAT EVERYONE NEEDS TO KNOW®

JAMES K. GALBRAITH

OXFORD

UNIVERSITY PRESS

OXFORD
UNIVERSITY PRESS

Oxford University Press is a department of the University of Oxford. It furthers the University's objective of excellence in research, scholarship, and education by publishing worldwide. Oxford is a registered trademark of Oxford University Press in the UK and certain other countries.

Published in the United States of America by Oxford University Press
198 Madison Avenue, New York, NY 10016, United States of America.

"What Everyone Needs to Know" is a registered trademark
of Oxford University Press.

© James K. Galbraith 2016

First Edition published in 2016

Cataloging-in-Publication data is on file at the Library of Congress
ISBN 978-0-19-025046-1 (hbk); 978-0-19-025047-8 (pbk)

1 3 5 7 9 8 6 4 2
Printed by RR Donnelley, USA

For Norman Birnbaum

CONTENTS

PREFACE

This small book crystallizes two decades of reflection and research on economic inequalities, since I was lured into the area by the debates over the roles of trade and technology that broke out in the mid-1990s. These years have seen the topic of inequality restored to the research agenda of many economists and to centrality in the public eye.

Both are mixed blessings. The public profile has created a simple political narrative to which there is a powerful inducement to conform. The attention of economists has fostered a host of competing theories, hypotheses, and assertions; what was once an uncluttered landscape is now a thicket, through which it is hard to see and even harder to cut a path. My goal is to give a tour of the most important issues, while keeping some distance from the polemics. No book on economic inequality can ever be strictly *apolitical*, but still—this is not a political book.

Throughout, I maintain two convictions. The first is that the history of economic ideas provides guidance on the principles. The problems are not new, and the texts that first tackled them, going back to Rousseau's *Discourse* and Adam Smith's *Wealth of Nations*, remain worth reading. The second is that an honest effort to sort through the facts requires the most careful attention to definition and measurement. For these reasons, readers will find chapters devoted to the history of ideas, concepts of pay and income, sources of data, and properties of particular measures.

My focus on evidence stems from the work of the University of Texas Inequality Project (UTIP) over many years. The work of this ever-changing group of talented graduate students has made a contribution to the systematic measurement of economic inequalities around the world, and so has made possible advances in the understanding of inequality as a matter of economic theory. They have lifted the curtain on a macroeconomics of inequality, and on the study of changing inequality as a function of forces affecting the world as a whole. I rely heavily on this work in what follows here, but I have kept the direct references down, until the very end, when there is a presentation of numbers.

This book is as non-technical as its subject permits, and as readable as I could make it. I have kept citations to a minimum; where a source is mentioned or relied on in the text, a reference is given at the end of the chapter. Readers who are interested in the mind-numbing varieties of inequality data that exist should consult the working paper "UTIP Global Inequality Data Sets 1963–2008" on the UTIP site at http://utip .gov.utexas.edu or in the working paper series of the United Nations University.

The format of the Oxford series "What Everyone Needs to Know" is to pose questions and provide answers. Never having attempted to write in this mode before, I found it engaging, and I hope that the same is true for the reader. I respect this format until the Epilogue and Appendix, which required a more direct approach.

Indeed there are some things about inequality that everyone needs to know. To find them, alongside just a few digressions, read on.

Austin, Texas
January 5, 2015

ACKNOWLEDGMENTS

This book owes its first debt to my student colleagues in the University of Texas Inequality Project, a long-running informal research group that has now led to some seven books, about seventy working papers, and a slew of refereed journal articles. UTIP has had perhaps twenty-five regular participants over the years; the present cohort consists of Jaehee Choi, Béatrice Halbach, Aleksandra Malinowska, Delfina Rossi, and Wenjie Zhang, along with Amin Shams, who did great work with us before moving along to study finance. They have contributed updated data sets, graphical and statistical analyses, teaching assistance, readings of the manuscript, and a weekly dose of conversation and common sense.

Let me thank also the talented students in my spring seminar these past few years on Development and Inequality at the LBJ School.

Lectures and conversations this past year or so with faculty, students, and conference participants at the Universities of Barcelona, Florence, and Rome, at the European Parliament, at UQAM and the Inequalities Summit at Montréal, at the World Knowledge Forum, Seoul National University and Konkuk University in Korea, at the Aalborg Post-Keynesian conference and CEVEA in Denmark, at the University of Missouri–Kansas City, the University of Science and Arts of Oklahoma, Michigan State University, St. John's University, Occidental

College, and the University of Wisconsin-Milwaukee have helped to focus my thinking and to ease the eventual passage of this book onto the page.

Scott Parris pressed hard to persuade me to write this book for Oxford University Press and showed great patience in the face of my initial reticence and prior commitments. Cathryn Vaulman and Prabhu Chinnasamy shepherded the manuscript into production, both with efficiency and skill. Dorothy Bauhoff copyedited with grace and precision. Two anonymous referees provided criticism and encouragement on the proposal. Wendy Strothman handled the contractual aspects with her usual wisdom. Michael Marder read the manuscript, caught some errors, and provided a raft of useful comments. Olivier Giovannoni graciously permitted me to use some of his graphical representations of changing inequality in the United States.

The work of UTIP has been supported by a generous grant from the Institute for New Economic Thinking, alongside the resources of the Lloyd M. Bentsen Jr. Chair in Government/ Business Relations, the facilities of the LBJ School, and the superb management of Lisa Johnson.

The year 2014 was one for many deep conversations on inequality and other topics that keep the mind fresh, including most especially with Bruno Amoroso, Norman Birnbaum, Andrea Cornia, Kari Polanyi Levitt, Michael Lind, Luigi Pasinetti, Giuseppe Sacco, and most especially and frequently with Yanis Varoufakis.

I want especially to acknowledge my new friend Giuseppe Guarino, a model of scholarship, integrity, and courage, who opened his home to my family and to me on two occasions.

This book was largely written during the month of December 2014, when most of my family was in China, save for Emma, who tackled the Franck Sonata while I typed away.

Finally, as ever, I'm grateful to Ying.

1

INEQUALITY

SHOULD WE CARE?

What Is Economic Inequality?

Equality—"we hold these truths to be self-evident, that all men are created equal"; "equal justice under law"; *liberté, egalité, fraternité*—is an ideal. Inequality, on the other hand, is our everyday reality, especially in the economic sphere. We sometimes deplore it. But we live with it, because we have to. The fact of inequality defines and shapes our lives. For most people—the exceptions are known to us as ascetics, widely admired but not much imitated—the fact of inequality generates the competition that determines status and standing and prestige and therefore success and failure in life.

Economic and social inequality takes many forms. *Class*—a group designation—is one of them; in former times it was more rigidly defined than it is now, but it is still present among us. *Rank* tells an individual's place in the scale of achievement, income, and power. *Wealth* is a concept that describes the financial valuation of personal or household possessions; it is a stock of things owned. *Income* is a flow of accessible resources, measured through time. Across nations, *citizenship* establishes a hierarchy of entitlement to common goods and protections, such as social insurance and health care. Within households, family and gender roles establish a hierarchy of power and privilege. Each of these is a dimension of inequality.

Economists tend to be especially interested in inequality of three types: pay, income, and wealth. That is not because these are necessarily the most important forms. Compared to (say) inequalities of race or gender, they may or may not be most closely tied (for instance) to stress, happiness, and the sense of justice or injustice. But we economists tend to study what we can most easily measure. And money is our measuring rod. It may be a warped and twisted rod—it is in fact both warped and twisted—but we use it because it's there. We use it in the hope that, by using it, we may discover something worth knowing of the world.

What Is the Inequality of Pay? What Is the Inequality of Income? What Is the Inequality of Wealth?

Pay and *earnings* are terms that refer to compensation for work. They encompass wages, which are usually paid on an hourly basis, and salaries, which are determined at an annual rate and do not depend on how many hours are actually worked. Benefits, bonuses, and deferred compensation may also be included in measures of pay. The inequality of pay, earnings, wages, and salaries reflects the pay rates in different jobs and the structure of jobs available in different societies. Industrial economists tend to focus on the relationship between the structure of industries and the distribution of pay. Labor economists often focus on the personal characteristics—race, gender, age, education—of those who hold the jobs.

Income is a broader concept. In addition to earnings, income includes such items as dividends, interest, royalties, realized capital gains, rental income, and transfer payments from the government such as unemployment insurance. The value of benefits such as food stamps may or may not be included; typically the value of a health insurance payout is not. National income accountants also have a concept of "imputed income," whose major component is the rental value of housing that is occupied by its owners. However, for the purposes of measuring inequality of incomes, the normal practice in most countries is to follow tax law: "income" is what the tax code requires you to report as income. In countries with no income tax, or where the income tax is weakly enforced, income statistics must rely on survey definitions that can vary according to the design of the survey—if surveys are taken at all.

Wealth is the value placed on a collection of possessions, or assets. Wealth includes financial assets, such as money, and stocks and bonds at their market value. It includes the value of houses, real estate, art, automobiles, jewelry and other possessions, net of any debts held against them. And it includes the capital value of present or future income flows, such as Social Security, Medicare, and Medicaid in the United States. Earnings and income are flows: they are measured over a period of time, such as a week, a month, or a year. Wealth is a stock, measured at any given moment of time. However, since there is no general tax on wealth, the rules for defining what is included and what is excluded are not strict. Sometimes people use a narrow definition, sometimes a broad one.

The inequality of pay or earnings is fairly easy to measure from available sources of data; payroll records are ubiquitous, and surveys of weekly or monthly earnings are widespread. Income inequality is also relatively easy to measure in countries with good surveys or good tax reporting. But there are not too many of the latter; the most impressive data set for tax incomes has just twenty-nine countries, strongly weighted toward the English-speaking world, so most income data are based on surveys. Wealth inequality is even harder to measure, and the results will vary depending on the definition of wealth in use; only a few countries survey wealth holdings officially. Holding of financial assets is unequal; most people do not accumulate financial wealth on a working income. Housing wealth is more broadly distributed, and Social Security wealth is widely held by working households, homeowners, and renters alike. But houses are hard to value, and Social Security wealth is often overlooked.

A paradox of study in this area holds that some of the things we care the most about are the most difficult to measure, and conversely, the things we find it easiest to measure are sometimes those about which we have relatively little reason to care.

What Has Happened in Recent Years to Economic Inequality in the United States and in the World?

Over the middle third of the twentieth century, inequality in most countries for which we have information—which isn't very many—tended to decline. For the United States, most sources agree that inequality peaked with the great stock market bubble of 1929, that it declined in the general impoverishment of the Great Depression and also in the recovery years of the New Deal, and that it declined sharply in the military mobilization for the Second World War. Thereafter the measures were more or less stable, with some further declines in the late 1960s under the impetus of the War on Poverty and the Great Society.

From around 1970 onward, pay and income inequalities in the United States started to rise. The increase became especially noticeable in the early 1980s—prompting initial congressional hearings, organized by this author, at the Joint Economic Committee in 1982. Around 1988, scholars began to take note as well, and since then the issue of rising inequality has become the subject of many lively debates. In very recent times, and especially in the aftermath of the Great Financial Crisis of 2008–2009, the rise in inequality has become a major political issue.

Is inequality still rising in the late 2010s? Some measures indicate that it is. Others are not so clear. Measures of pay inequality in the United States, for instance, seem to have peaked in the early 1990s, and to have declined as the economy reached full employment in the late 1990s. Measures of income inequality—which include dividends and realized capital gains, as well as the salaries and bonuses of top executives in finance and technology—reached a peak in 2000, with the end of the information-technology boom. Thereafter these measures show a sawtooth pattern closely corresponding to asset price movements, notably the real estate–finance bubble peaking in 2007, and the stock market recovery beginning in 2010. Measures differ on whether the most recent values are little higher, or a little lower, than 2000. In any event, it is clear that the great rise of US income inequality became less certain and inexorable after 2000 than it was before.

The trend—if any—in the world as a whole has been much harder to observe. There is no world statistics agency that collects information on incomes at the global scale, and so evidence on this question is a matter of piecing together the available measures for individual countries. There are many such measures, but they are not consistent with each other, and a simple comparison can make it very difficult to find a trend. However, other techniques can be brought to bear, and at least one such effort—my own—does find a common pattern for pay and income inequalities within countries, around the world. The pattern shows approximate stability in the 1960s, a general decline in inequalities in much of the world in the 1970s, and then a long sharp rise after 1980, cascading around the world from Latin America to Central Europe to Asia, and (as in the United States) peaking in 2000. Thereafter, the evidence at hand suggests modestly declining inequalities in important parts of the world, including Russia, much of South America, and, most recently, in China after 2008.

There are many qualifications that may be made to the previous paragraph, but we will leave them, for now, until a later part of this book.

Why Is Economic Inequality Important?

To many people, the importance of economic inequalities seems self-evident. To the person who is poor, the difficulty and the remedy are both quite clear: one hasn't enough and one needs more. All the more so, if that person belongs to a group that suffers discrimination or has so suffered in the past. It is similarly evident for those who sympathize with those who are poor or discriminated against. Reducing economic inequalities will mean, in general, fewer people who fall far below the norms of that society, and that low-income groups will also not be so far below the standard set by more privileged groups.

Does this mean that reducing inequalities also reduces poverty and discrimination? As a matter of logic, the answer has to be *not necessarily*. Reducing inequalities may incur an economic cost: the more-equal society may be poorer, on average, than it was before, with the misery shared by all. A political revolution that eliminates (or drives into exile) a prior elite can have this quality. The resulting society may (or may not) be less oppressive than the one it overthrew, but given the disruptions and violence that go along with revolution, it is unlikely to be wealthier on average, at least at first. The experience of communism was, for many people, an experience of hardship.

In a similar vein, it is possible to reduce inequalities without reducing discrimination. It may be the case that after a reduction of inequality, for instance, a particular group (women, racial minorities) has exactly the same position as before, at the bottom of the economic ladder. The ladder may be shorter than it was. Poverty and hardship may be less, while discrimination remains unchanged. The leaders and members of an excluded group may accept the absolute gains they have achieved, as a kind of substitute for achieving equal treatment alongside favored groups. Or, they may not. Material well-being and social justice overlap, but they are not the same thing.

An important question is whether inequalities have good or bad effects on the overall economic and social performance of an economic system. We all agree that some degree of inequality is essential—and that being so, it is practically inevitable that some groups will persistently have higher incomes and wealth, on average, than some others. But when, if ever, is the degree of inequality too much? This cannot be a question answered only from the perspective of those at the bottom; it has to take as its point of view the standpoint of the society or system as a whole.

Obviously, this issue is very controversial! Standard theories in economics have tried for decades to explain the degree of inequality present in an economy as a function of external facts, such as the requirements of technological change or the expansion of world trade. They thus argue, in effect, that inequality is not really something that we can influence or should be directly concerned about. If these theories were correct, they would spare us from examining the degree of inequality in the economic system, at least from the standpoint of economic performance. However, in this economist's view, the theories are not broadly persuasive and there seems to be no alternative to thinking of inequalities as something societies construct, in the main, for themselves.

How is inequality constructed? In part—as the great Scottish economist Adam Smith wrote in the eighteenth century—societies do it by creating legal and social privileges: essentially protections, subsidies, and monopoly power. In part, as Karl Marx wrote in the nineteenth century, capitalism does it by a process of exploitation, extracting surplus value from the working masses. In part, as Joseph Schumpeter wrote in the early twentieth century, technological change does it by extending large prizes to those who manage to make fundamental transformations in the way we live our lives. Some of these forces are useful; others are unavoidable; still others are dangerous and require management and control.

And how do modern societies reduce inequality? In part by regulation, including direct regulation of wages, prices, and interest rates. In part by taxation. In part by providing public infrastructure and consumption goods, in which all share. And in part by social insurance, which assures a minimum income to those displaced by economic change or sidelined by age or illness. Again, whether all of these forces and institutions are well run and necessary is a matter of unending dispute.

Do battles over distribution and redistribution affect economic performance? Conflict itself is costly. Physical violence is destructive. Strikes and lockouts affect production. Inflation—sometimes seen as a consequence of unresolved distributive struggle—is a distraction from normal economic life. Consensus, collaboration, and peace are productive. However, they are not always possible to achieve.

Conventional economic theory tends to argue that in modern times, economic efficiency has favored more unequal societies, including the United States. Why? Mainly because higher technology (it is said) requires greater skills, which in turn are properly compensated at higher rates. So a more unequal society experiencing rapid technological change should (on balance) have less unemployment than a society that maintains "rigid labor markets" with high wages paid to unskilled workers and big obstacles to hiring and firing employees.

Other theories and empirical research have challenged this argument. For example, it may be that nations with high inequalities in available pay have more unemployment, simply because more people abandon low-wage jobs (say on a Chinese farm) in order to take their chances (say in construction in Chinese cities). It seems obvious that the huge inequalities between town and country in many nations spur internal migration and job search, just as huge inequalities between countries spur international migration. Empirical work also seems to suggest the opposite of the conventional view.

Countries with relatively low inequality in pay structures—such as in Scandinavia—tend to have systematically higher productivity and lower unemployment rates than their more unequal neighbors and competitors. And it may be that societies perceived as unfair, and untrustworthy, just don't work as well. An eloquent argument of this type against American inequality has been given, most recently, by Joseph Stiglitz.

In a formal democracy, another aspect of extreme economic inequality is the power that devolves on the very rich. Adam Smith wrote, "wealth, as Mr. Hobbes says, is power." *As Mr. Hobbes says*—The high inequality that has come to characterize the United States in recent decades has meant unequal access to political power, in part for the simple reason that winning elections requires money. This aspect of inequality ties economics to politics, in a way that is hard to dismiss or avoid.

In the great sweep of international comparisons, another basic fact bears notice. It is the case that richer societies tend to be more equal than poorer societies. And why is this? The answer is intuitive and straightforward. A rich society, *by definition*, must have a large middle class. That is, it must have many individuals and families owning a significant share of the national bounty. It is not possible for a rich country—the very exceptional case of small oil sheikhdoms apart—to have its national wealth tied up in the hands of a tiny group of princes, nobles, or knights. The poorer countries of the world are precisely those where economic activity is divided sharply between small numbers with control of valuable resources (including land), and much larger numbers of the impoverished and dispossessed.

So the processes of economic development almost invariably produce lower inequalities over time; and along with lower inequalities come the benefits that we associate with civilized life: public pensions, health insurance, free public education, national parks, and cultural amenities. The issue within the development process is whether it is a good or a bad idea to try to accelerate the movement toward equality. An issue for rich countries, who have already achieved relatively low inequality, is whether the wealth brought the reduction of inequality—or whether the reduction of inequalities brought the wealth.

And having said that, notice that so far, we have only discussed the question of whether higher or lower economic inequality is a good or a bad thing. But what about changes in the level of inequality? Is rising inequality a bad thing? Is falling inequality a good thing? We observe in the last generation, up to the most recent few years, that in many rich and poor countries alike, inequality has risen. Is this a new phase in their development, perhaps associated, in the case of the rich, with new and advanced forms of technical change? Or is it a sign of development going into reverse, and of rising inequality threatening the social gains of the past half-century or more?

This, too, is not an easy question, and it may not have a single answer. If inequality is too low, stifling enterprise and innovation, why not let it rise? If it is too high, sparking a sense of injustice, why not bring it down? Or, as in the famous case of the Chinese reform process after 1976, why not let it rise at first and (maybe) bring it back down later? The answer may depend entirely on context. In some situations, reducing inequality may be the correct economic policy; in others, perhaps it should be allowed to rise. And yet, despite all these qualifications, we may still care.

The philosopher John Rawls suggested a reason that it is reasonable to care about the level of inequality in the abstract. Suppose, he argued, one had to choose the general degree of inequality in society from behind a "veil of ignorance," that is, without knowing one's own position in that society? Then one would rationally choose a society that was not excessively unequal—and in which inequalities were justified only to the degree that they lifted up the poorest and most vulnerable citizens. To the extent that we can detach ourselves from our actual position, and indulge Rawls's thought experiment, we can appreciate that inequality matters, even if it is in some respects unavoidable and, in some instances and within limits, actually to be desired.

2

INEQUALITY IN THE HISTORY OF ECONOMIC THOUGHT

We in the United States are accustomed to the principle that "all men are created equal." But of course that principle is not from time immemorial; it is not "self-evident" even now, and was far from being so, to most people, at the time it was written. It was part of a revolutionary document—the Declaration of Independence—because it embodied a revolutionary sentiment, worthy of note in the climate of the time. So we need to adjust our minds to the fact that *inequality* is the immemorial state of the human species, as it is of virtually all other social species, from ants to mountain gorillas.

Against this backdrop, the assertion of a fundamental norm of *equality* is the noteworthy development, which requires a word of explanation. And the history of political economy, from that time to the present, can be seen in good part as a contest between the egalitarian ideal and the unequal reality, between a felt need to pursue the former and a felt need to accept and even justify the latter.

Whence the Idea of Equality?

In his 1755 essay entitled "Discourse on the Origin of Inequality," the French philosopher Jean-Jacques Rousseau located the rise of inequality in the creation of property rights. Rousseau wrote: "as there is scarce any inequality among men in a state of nature, all that which we now behold owes its force and its growth to the development of our faculties and the improvement of our understanding, and at last becomes permanent and lawful by the establishment of property and of laws."

Rousseau's "state of nature" was a mental construct, intended to represent neither human history nor the actual aboriginal societies in America and elsewhere. It was an abstraction, whose purpose was to illustrate that in an asocial setting— a hypothetical forest of hunters and gatherers—human differences would be limited to personal physical and mental characteristics. In that setting, any effort to subordinate or enslave one person to any other would always fail, since the person in the lower position could get up and leave at any time. Therefore the modern state of hierarchy and order could arise only within a frame of compulsion and law, to which people were bound and from which they could not escape. Slavery is a tight form of such binding; citizenship, or "freedom," is a looser form, but a variation nevertheless on the theme. Not many people, even today, escape from the national legal framework into which they were born, and those who do, only enter another one, equally binding.

Rousseau was not content to accept social inequalities as they are. Having perceived their origin, he then wrote: "it likewise follows that moral inequality, authorized by any right that is merely positive, clashes with natural right ... a distinction which sufficiently determines, what we are able to think in that respect of that kind of inequality which obtains in all civilized nations, since it is evidently against the law of nature that infancy should command old age, folly conduct wisdom, and a handful of men should choke with superfluities, while the famished multitude want the commonest necessities of life."

"Evidently against the law of nature"—words like that can motivate rebellion, revolution, and even the guillotine. However, since we necessarily live in society, it is not quite clear how far the law of nature should rule. Rousseau set a tough standard. Political economists ever since have tried to explain (and justify) actual existing economic inequalities, in actual existing human societies, in terms that might blunt the sharp edge of the philosopher's blade.

How Did Economics Come to View Inequality as the Product of Natural Law?

In 1776 the Scottish moral philosopher Adam Smith published his great treatise, *An Inquiry into the Nature and Causes of the Wealth of Nations*. It is in many ways a strikingly modern, practical book, full of current observation and historical digression, as well as being a systematic attempt to elucidate the principles of economic life.

Smith was a product of the merchant and colonial era, following the Glorious Revolution of 1688 in England, and in his society—in contrast to Rousseau's France—the feudal distinctions of class, as between king, lords, and commoners, were still present but no longer paramount. They were in the course of being erased by the rise of a new commercial (and soon, industrial) class, later to be called the bourgeoisie. Smith therefore had a new problem to solve, namely the principles underlying the division of the "annual revenue" of a country between three classes that were not *necessarily* fixed and hereditary: workers, who earn wages; masters, who earn the profits of "stock" or capital; and landlords, who own land and earn rent. Much of the first part of Smith's book is preoccupied with this problem, to which his solutions were not highly satisfactory to later writers. Still, they helped to frame a major source of economic inequality, what economists now call the *functional distribution of income*.

What Is the Functional Distribution of Income?

Long before there were any measures of household or personal income, or any income tax systems or surveys that would permit us to measure such things, classical political economy divided the economic world into major classes, just as the feudal world had been, and the differences between these classes were a matter of categorical inequalities, to be discussed more generally in Chapter 3. However, the categories in question were not those of race or gender (as we use today), nor were they the categories of sovereign, lord, priest, peasant, and serf that had been predominant in medieval times.

Instead, classical economics specified three basic orders: capitalists, workers, and landlords. These orders earned incomes each of a fundamentally special type, peculiar to itself: profits, wages, and rents. The laws of classical political economy were thus largely taken up with determining the principles of the division of income into these three types, and today we refer to that division as the *functional distribution of income*.

The principles of the functional distribution included a competitive theory of profits (which could be distorted by monopolies) with a general tendency toward a declining rate of profit on new investments over time. The theory of wages that evolved over the nineteenth century was designed mostly to explain why wages would never rise, whether because of population pressure or exploitation. When wages did rise, the classical theory was displaced by the modern neoclassical version, which held that labor received a share of output in proportion to its contribution to the production of output at the margin—this is the concept of *marginal productivity*. Instead of conflict and misery, the neoclassical theory proposed that the factors of production worked in a cooperative spirit, each in its place, and shared the rewards in proportion to their contributions.

Land was believed by the classics to yield a rent in proportion to its relative capacity to produce—in comparison with the barren land at the margin of cultivation, or distant suburbs at the margin of urban settlement. Since land cannot be reproduced, and is ultimately scarce, classical economists believed that the landlords would remain the most richly rewarded group, and they proposed that effective taxation would be levied on the value of land. Neoclassical economics tended to forget about land—partly because landlords may have wanted to be forgotten—and in the twentieth century the functional distribution of income came to describe the division of national income between capital and labor.

In the mid-twentieth century there arose a body of formal economic theory that placed the functional distribution into a mathematical framework, and derived precise expressions for the marginal productivities of capital and labor under various assumptions about the state of technology and technique. This gave rise to an important question: In what units were labor (L) and capital (K) to be measured? Labor could, in a pinch, be viewed as a measure of time, that is, of hours worked (overlooking entirely the issue of the quality of work by different persons). But capital? There is no natural unit for physical quantities of highly heterogeneous machines and process-goods, and counting up dollars invested doesn't work, since it requires a depreciation formula, which requires an interest rate, which is the rate of profit one is trying to derive! The "Cambridge controversies" on this topic raged for about a decade, at which point (in 1966) Paul Samuelson of MIT conceded that one could not legitimately use aggregate capital in a production function. But then something odd happened: most economists went on doing just that, as if the fallacy of counting up machines by the money spent on them had never been uncovered.

Fifty years later, a theory of the functional distribution that is derived from a "production function" using capital and labor as the inputs to production remains a mainstay of economics textbooks. This reflects the power of category-building on the human mind, at least in economics. For why should we think in terms of machinery and inventories as forming a coherent categorical structure called "capital"—or anything else—and why should we think of all time spent on the job as the performance of a common function called "labor"? In many ways, both of these phenomena are so diverse that no comparability within them exists; there is neither a meaningful measure of labor nor of capital.

The functional distribution can be thought of as that part of inequality explained, if not actually justified, by the operation of economic principles. Thus the *wages* workers earn are explained by their education, skill, seniority, the danger of the job, its prestige, and other factors. What merchants and factory owners earn is governed by competition of capitals, leading to a uniform *rate of profit*. What landlords earn, known as *rent*, is governed by the fertility of the soils that they happen to own. The results may be unequal, but they are, at least, established by the functioning of markets. And so, for that reason, they are not "against the laws of nature." To the contrary, for Smith and his contemporaries, the economic laws that established wages, profits, and rent were, in effect, laws of nature.

The functional distribution—and especially the division of income between profits and wages—remains embedded in our national income accounts and in our politics—a legacy of the struggles between Marxist and neoclassical economic traditions over the role of these categories in the fate of capitalist society. So it is not likely to go away. Figure 2.1 gives a picture of the labor share in US income from 1929 to 2012. It shows that the overall share of labor has remained stable. However, within that share, the portion taken by a small number at the top of the earnings distribution has risen dramatically. The stable labor share in total income is, therefore, cold comfort for many American workers, and it is the shape of the distribution that likely matters most. We will return to the shape of distributions in Chapter 4.

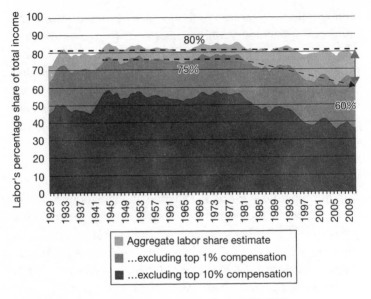

Figure 2.1 Share of Labor in National Income, United States, 1929–2012
Credit: Olivier Giovannoni. Used with permission.

What Were the "Inequalities Occasioned by the Policies of Europe?"

As we have seen, Smith accepted inequalities given by "nature." What he objected to were laws of society that prevented the laws of nature from functioning as well as they might. In his own country, there were still many artifacts of the feudal age, enshrined in the statutes of the realm, and these—especially those having to do with bounties, tariffs, guilds, apprenticeships, and efforts to keep gold and silver from going "forth of the kingdom"—Smith attacked with verve and gusto. He was even more incensed, however, by what he observed across the channel, mainly in France, which he called "Inequalities occasioned by the policy of Europe."

What were these? They were in a word, *monopolies*. Smith wrote, "The policy of Europe occasions a very important inequality in the whole of the advantages and disadvantages of the different employments of labour and stock, by restraining the competition in some employments to a smaller number than might otherwise be disposed to enter them. The exclusive privileges of corporations are the principal means it makes use of for this purpose." *Corporations* in Smith's day was a word generally referring to towns, not companies, but Smith also had this to say about tradesmen: "People of the same trade seldom meet together, even for merriment and diversion, but the conversation ends in a conspiracy against the public, or in some contrivance to raise prices."

Smith's point was one that we still struggle with in our own time. The protections of the state, for private enterprises of all types—and perhaps especially in our day for banks—is surely one of the greatest sources of economic inequality, and the one most clearly in violation of "nature's laws." And most economists to this day still believe in the elixir of competition as a cure—notwithstanding how seldom that remedy seems ever to have been applied.

What Was the Iron Law of Wages, and Why Did Malthus and Ricardo and Their Contemporaries Believe That the Poor Could Not and Should Not Be Helped?

As the nineteenth century and the industrial revolution rolled in, factory wage-labor became the socially dominant form, at least in England, where David Ricardo, a Jewish financier, and Thomas Robert Malthus, an Anglican cleric, dominated the development of economic theory. Much of their effort was given over to working out more exact principles for the functional distribution of income, and especially for theories of wages and rent. Here Malthus made the key contribution to a theory of wages, while Ricardo clarified the theory of rent and its difference from the theory of profit.

Factory wage labor was something quite new. In feudal times tenant farmers shared their harvest with the lord and church, while artisans sold the products that they crafted with their own tools. Under industrial capitalism, however, former farmers and former craftsmen were stripped of land and tools; they entered the master's shop with nothing but the shirt on their backs. And they were paid wages, not according to their physical output, but by the hour—according to time.

Malthus's theory of wages was in essence a simple relationship between the supply of labor and the supply of food. He argued that population would grow at a geometric rate, while the capacity of the land to feed that population would grow, at best, at a lower "arithmetic" rate. Hence the working population would always be rubbing up against the available food supply, and the *real wage* or living standard of the working person could never rise far above the subsistence level. If it did, famine, pestilence, and war were available to knock the population back down. This was the Iron Law of Wages. It was not a happy prospect for the workers, but then, the miserable material conditions in factory towns were apparent confirmation of Malthus's idea.

How Did Ricardo Distinguish Profit from Rent?

One of Ricardo's signal contributions was a coherent explanation of the rent of land. Rent, he argued, depended on the extent of cultivation, and on the difference between the fertility of any given piece of land and the *worst* land then under tillage. Why so? Because, Ricardo reasoned, while the worst land in use would not yield any rent, it would still have to repay, at the going price of grain, the labor required to till it and a normal profit on the equipment required for the work. All other land would have similar labor and profit requirements, but higher yields related to the superior fertility, irrigation, and location of the soil. This the landlord could demand for himself. Thus rent at any time would depend on two factors: the differential productivity of the soil, and the price of the final product, which would determine just how much land would (at any time) come under cultivation. (Rent, in turn, had no effect on price in Ricardo's theory.)

Ricardo's theory of rent and Malthus's theory of wages were the dominant ideas in a great debate of that era, over the repeal of the "Corn Laws," which were Napoleonic-era English tariffs on the importation of wheat. Landlords favored the tariffs, since expensive wheat meant high rents and good incomes for them, according to Ricardo's theory. Emerging capitalists opposed them, because cheaper wheat from Ireland and America meant they could pay an expanding workforce at a lower price. But an interesting implication of Malthus's theory was that the price of wheat—the basic staple of the wage bill—*made no difference to the workers*. They would be paid a subsistence quantity of wheat, whatever price was paid for it on the larger market; their wages would fall (in money terms) if the price of their consumption also fell. Hence as the issue was debated in Parliament—and the Corn Laws were eventually repealed—it was not felt necessary to consult those who ate the corn.

Why Did Karl Marx Believe That Capitalism Generates Only Poverty for Workers?

The nineteenth century saw a great wave of industrialization and tumultuous economic change around the world, but the epicenter long remained in Great Britain, where the German refugee and political activist Karl Marx spent his days in the reading room of the British Museum, drafting the monumental work of theory and polemic known as *Capital*.

Marx rejected the Malthusian doctrine of the Iron Law. It was obvious, by his day, that there were no biological limits to production. The triumph of bourgeois capitalism had broken through all previous productivity records, creating for the first time a vast outpouring of cheap manufactured goods, while new lands and world trade were at the same time reducing the cost of growing food. But why then were workers still so poor? Why were they ground down, as Marx documented in great detail from parliamentary commissions and other investigative records, to a status no better than slaves, their health broken by overwork, dust, toxic chemicals, and dangerous machinery?

Marx's answer rooted wages in a theory of exploitation. Consider that even under the most productive and efficient system, workers must work a certain number of hours each day, merely to produce the goods necessary to feed themselves and their families in the most minimal way. Marx called that time commitment the value of *labor-power*. But then, there is the rest of the working day, during which workers produce over and above what they themselves must be paid. What happens to that production? Under capitalism, it remains the property of the capitalist who owns the machinery, the factory, and the process-goods. Marx called the time devoted to producing these extra goods a measure of *surplus value*.

It's obvious that the capitalist has an interest in getting as much surplus value out of the worker as possible. Much of *Capital* is devoted to cataloging the ways that this may be done. Long working days, long working weeks, harsh conditions, women's labor, child labor—the examples, from textile mills and coal mines to lacemaking shops to the fine potteries of Staffordshire, make for grim reading even today. To Marx, this was not a matter of mere greed, sadism, or other wickedness. On the contrary, capitalists were obliged, by the brute facts of competition with other capitalists, to treat their workers as miserably as possible. Competition assured that only the most brutal would survive. Vast inequality and conflict between the classes were therefore inescapable features of the system.

The problem for capitalism, if Marx was right, was how to sell the vast production of all the new factories. Capitalists, a small group, could never, even at their most extravagant, consume their own share. And if workers were being paid only the minimum necessary for subsistence, then by definition they would never have the purchasing power required to absorb the output. The solution could only be to absorb the surplus output in paying for new investments—which do not immediately yield consumption goods—or in exports, or in war. Exports in those protectionist days required colonies as a protected market, hence the British took over India in part as a dumping ground for cheap Manchester cottons, while the British and French together waged war on China to force open its markets to opium, a product of British India and French Indochina that the Chinese did not want. Later, in the First World War, the surplus industrial production of the European Great Powers would find its outlet in the machines that produced the systematic slaughter of millions of young men.

Marx, of course, hoped for a different result, namely a communist revolution. "This integument is burst asunder. The knell of private property sounds. The expropriators are expropriated." Such was his answer to Rousseau.

In What Way, Did Keynes Argue, Was Inequality Actually Responsible for the Success of Capitalism in the Late Nineteenth Century?

While Marx developed his theory of inequality-leading-to-revolution, actually things were looking up for the working classes of Europe. Bit by bit, over the second half of the nineteenth century, living standards began to rise. Perhaps the gap between rich and poor was as great as ever—the period came to be known in the United States as the Gilded Age. But the pall of grinding mass poverty began to lift, and both the Iron Law and Marx's theory of maximum surplus value began to come under question.

It was the young John Maynard Keynes, born in 1883—the year Marx died—who eloquently captured the spirit of the late nineteenth century in the opening pages of his essay, *The Economic Consequences of the Peace*, written in furious protest against the terms of the Versailles Treaty of 1919. At the beginning of that small book, Keynes offered a few words on the fading Malthusian question in the fifty years before the Great War.

> That happy age lost sight of a view of the world which filled with deep-seated melancholy the founders of our Political Economy. Before the eighteenth century mankind entertained no false hopes. To lay the illusions which grew popular at that age's latter end, Malthus disclosed a Devil. For half a century all serious economical writings held that Devil in clear prospect. For the next half century he was chained up and out of sight.

In Keynes's view, part of the gains of the working classes in the prewar era were owed to the still-greater gains of the business leaders—*provided* that those leaders, the capitalists, made appropriate use of their gains by investing them rather than burning them up in high living. Keynes's section on the "psychology of society" deserves to be quoted at some length.

> The new rich of the nineteenth century were not brought up to large expenditures, and preferred the power which investment gave them to the pleasures of immediate consumption. In fact, it was precisely the *inequality* of the distribution of wealth which made possible those vast accumulations of fixed wealth and of capital improvements which distinguished that age from all others. Herein lay, in fact, the main justification of the Capitalist System. If the rich had spent their new wealth on their own enjoyments, the world would long ago have found such a régime intolerable. But like bees they saved and accumulated, not less to the advantage of the whole community because they themselves held narrower ends in prospect. . . .

Thus this remarkable system depended for its growth on a double bluff or deception. On the one hand the laboring classes accepted from ignorance or powerlessness, or were compelled, persuaded, or cajoled by custom, convention, authority, and the well-established order of Society into accepting, a situation in which they could call their own very little of the cake that they and Nature and the capitalists were co-operating to produce. And on the other hand the capitalist classes were allowed to call the best part of the cake theirs and were theoretically free to consume it, on the tacit underlying condition that they consumed very little of it in practice.

Thus the "happy age" that arose under Queen Victoria and ended in August 1914—Keynes's analysis of those lost years captures the spirit of many who are still nostalgic for the "Victorian virtues" of frugality and thrift. However, there were others who looked at those years from a quite different perspective, and of these, the greatest was an American, the economist Thorstein Veblen.

What Was Veblen's Theory of the Leisure Class?

While the young Keynes waxed lyrical about the "double bluff" that had turned rising inequalities into a cornucopia of productivity and rising living standards for the working population of Europe, across the Atlantic a scholar of considerably more cynical disposition was studying the new rich of America's Gilded Age. This was Thorstein Veblen, whose *Theory of the Leisure Class* first appeared in 1899, to the great discomfort of the "higher barbarians" of whom it made sport. "Conspicuous consumption," "conspicuous leisure," "conspicuous waste," and "pecuniary emulation" are among the phrases coined here that still are sometimes heard today.

Veblen had no truck with the notion that to be a capitalist was a form of work: "the characteristic feature of leisure class life is a conspicuous exemption from all useful employment." In Veblen's view, the "work" of the wealthy consists largely of finding imaginative ways to advertise the fact of that exemption. In this way, and by displaying the properties that naturally accompany great wealth, the wealthy earn their prestige.

Property, Veblen pointed out, began with the ownership of women, and extended next to slaves, and thence to the accumulation of personal material possessions. As these became important, the greatest prestige would accrue to the ownership of the most useless, rare, fanciful, and decorated objects; by the personal consumption of the richest foods, most expensive liquors, the fanciest and most dangerous poisons; by the maintenance of the largest and most elaborate households, including expensive and useless pets; and by the putting on of the most lavish entertainments—thus oil paintings, cognacs, cigars, chihuahuas, and masked balls. In our day, Veblen might have added the lure of competitive philanthropy as a status game for the very rich.

Veblen's Leisure Class proper consisted mainly of four major orders: the government, priests, athletes, and warriors. Each has its own status systems and symbols, driven by a combination of money and other rewards, especially ranks and honors. Professors form a junior tributary or symbolic offshoot of the priesthood. Ceremony, handed down from medieval times and earlier, continues to pervade the life of these orders, and the devotion to ceremonial achievement distinguishes them from those who have to work for a living. Needless to say, the leisure class is a direct descendant of the early hunting man-pack, and its dominant participants are (to this day) overwhelmingly male. Indeed the institution of the Leisure Class is roughly coterminous with the general power of human males over human females.

And, as Veblen observed, useful work is precisely the province, in the main, of women. Women's propensity to labor stems from their role in earlier times as the tillers of

the fields; while men hunted, women farmed. Hunting therefore carried prestige, and farming did not. In the modern
world, while men compete for status, women actually run the
machinery in factories, sell the goods in shops, and manage
consumption in the home. All of that, though the essential
stuff of economic life, is—by social construction—drudgery.

To Veblen the pivotal players for the survival of this system were neither capitalists nor workers, but the engineers. It
was they who (on behalf of their masters) kept the machinery
of industry in gear. So where Marx sought the overthrow of
an unequal system, and where the young Keynes lamented
its fallen effectiveness as a source of rising prosperity for all,
Veblen saw no way out of the world dominated by the leisure
class—except, *possibly*, through what he called a "Soviet of
Engineers." But, as he realized, it was easy enough to keep the
engineers placid, well-fed, and accepting of their lot—today
in America this is done, in part, by importing them from less-
favored lands, and maintaining them on provisional visas—
and so a revolution against the leisure class remained, then as
now, unlikely.

Why Did Joseph Schumpeter Reject Concern over Inequality, and Argue (to the Contrary) That Too Much Bother over Inequalities Was Actually the Greater Danger?

Into the intellectual climate framed by Veblen in America
in the 1920s, there appeared our next protagonist, a former
Austrian finance minister turned Harvard professor named
Joseph Schumpeter. A brilliant archconservative, Schumpeter
rejected both the egalitarian textbook fantasy of competitive
economic theory and the egalitarian social idealism of the
followers of Veblen and Marx. Instead, he argued that large
inequalities were not only to be tolerated, but that they are
actually essential.

For Schumpeter the advantage of great wealth did not lie
in a disciplined propensity to save and invest. He was not

an admirer of the rich, however disciplined they might have been. Instead he admired the ambitious and the greedy. What mattered was the *prospect* of enormous economic gains. In an advanced country, these could be had in one way, better than all others: by constructing a new enterprise around some new technology, with transient economic power, thanks to a successful innovation. Great fortunes arise from capitalizing the prospects for future sales, thanks to this achievement.

Yet innovation, as Schumpeter realized, is a two-edged sword. On one side, it reduces costs and increases consumption possibilities, so living standards can improve. But on the other side, successful innovation necessarily destroys the firms and industries that it displaces. It therefore supplants a stable, mature, competitive, egalitarian production network with its opposite: a production node that is highly unequal, monopolistic, and unstable. Schumpeter called this process "creative destruction." For him it was the distinctive motor of capitalist progress.

The advantage of having a few great prizes was that this would motivate a large number of people to seek them, each one overestimating his chances. The result would be vast gains to the winners, but also large numbers of disappointed and defeated might-have-beens, and vast inequalities between them. But there would also be social and material dynamism. The achievement of capitalism, Schumpeter wrote, does not lie in providing silk stockings for queens, but in making them available to factory girls in return for steadily decreasing effort. If money wages are maintained as a stable share of total output (which Schumpeter saw as the normal condition of capitalist distribution), that would ensure that declining prices of ever-better output translate into a rising standard of living for the working class.

Schumpeter, like Marx and against Keynes, was pessimistic about the prospect for highly unequal capitalism to survive. But his reasons were very different. The danger, as he saw it, came not from the contradictions and conflicts of capital and labor, but from the state, and especially from bureaucracy and regulation, acting in a democratic system as the agent of the working classes. If the state were to muffle private incentives in the name of the general welfare, then Schumpeter feared that innovation and change would be suppressed. For what is the point of taking a big risk, if the prize is not enormous?

Schumpeter therefore opposed Franklin Roosevelt's New Deal and, more generally, Keynes's program to fight the Great Depression with public spending. He was confident that depressions work themselves out; they came and went with waves of creative destruction. But even if one disagrees about that—as the American public under FDR certainly did—one can still make a case that in principle Schumpeter had a point. To take the extreme example, many hold that bureaucracy, regulation, and central planning contributed to poor work effort and to the technical deficiencies of much production and distribution of goods and services in the Soviet Union, especially toward the end. Socialism may be fair, but capitalism is dynamic, and Schumpeter's followers argue that dynamism wins out in the end, every time.

Did Simon Kuznets Have the Final Word?

The final great figure in our survey will be Simon Kuznets, an American of Russian extraction who won a Nobel Prize in Economics in 1971. Kuznets had many distinctions; he was an inventor of National Income Accounting in the 1930s, and in the 1940s he played a central role in working out materiel requirements for US production in the Second World War. After the war he turned his attention to economic development. In 1955 he was president of the American Economic Association, and in that capacity delivered the most influential lecture on development and inequality ever given.

Unlike Veblen, Kuznets was not a social critic. Unlike Marx, Keynes, Schumpeter, or Stiglitz, he was not especially concerned with the consequences of inequalities as a scientific matter. Instead, Kuznets wanted to understand the driving forces behind changing *degrees* of inequality, especially over the course of economic development. And so he offered a very simple hypothesis.

Suppose the starting point for economic development is a country of small farmers, as in parts of pre-industrial Britain or the North of the United States. Such a society will be relatively egalitarian; one small farmer is rarely much richer or much poorer than his neighbor. But then, suppose that a process of industrial and urban development gets under way. Factory jobs invariably pay more than the surrounding farms; they have to, or people will not move to town. Cities are also internally unequal; they have bankers and they have people to sweep the streets. Hence as cities develop, inequality must rise. It will rise, Kuznets reasoned, up to a certain point, when there is a general balance of population between urban and rural regions, and at that point, it will reach a maximum value. Afterward, as the population becomes mostly urban, the city-country difference becomes less important, and inequality must decline. Also, as cities develop, Kuznets believed they would be subject to the pressures of social democracy and would become, internally, less unequal. On both counts the general pattern would be an inverted *U*, with inequality rising early in the development process and declining later on.

Kuznets's work has been taken by some as intended to rationalize rising inequality in the course of capitalist development, and there may have been an element of that in the climate of the 1950s. But it is mostly a deep, yet common-sense, historical analysis—which does not mean that it is necessarily always true. Many economists since Kuznets have looked for inverted *U*-curves in income and development data, and usually with little success. This only proves that it is possible to publish papers while systematically missing the point.

In the starting conditions of the American plantation South, for instance, inequalities could scarcely have been higher. The region might have become steadily more equal as slavery was abolished and eventually industrial development took hold; one would not expect to find the inverted U-curve there. In the conditions of the modern United States, with a large financial and high-technology sector, inequalities might *rise*, instead of fall, with more rapid economic growth. That is because a large share of top incomes in the United States derive directly or indirectly from capital markets. In an oil sheikhdom, on the other hand, inequalities may vary with the price of oil.

The patterns therefore differ, but the general insight of Kuznets remains compelling. We should expect changes in inequality to reflect the changing distribution of the population across regions and economic activities, and the changing relationship of regions and sectors to each other. A very decent share of changing inequality in measures from countries around the world over the course of economic development should be explainable by these simple processes—and only after accounting for them should it become necessary to seek out the more exotic explanations.

3

CATEGORICAL INEQUALITY

There is another way to think about inequalities. And that is to classify individuals into groups to which they belong, and look at the inequalities that exist between various groups, usually between the average (or median) income (or pay, or wealth) of one group as compared with another. These cases are called *categorical inequalities* and they are a powerful force in all human societies.

Categorical schemes—or *taxonomies*—cannot be created a priori; they must be based on something—such as properties or measurements, or in the case of biological categories, kinship and common heritage in an evolutionary tree. The botanical tables of Linnaeus were a beauty and a marvel, but since they classified plants and flowers by physical similarity, they were not a reliable guide to closeness in evolutionary terms. What to do instead when faced with the grouping problem in economics? The categorical schemes of classical and neoclassical economics were based on the theoretical concepts of labor, capital, and land—and they stand or fall on that system of accounts. But suppose most people have some income from each of these categories, so that the lines of demarcation are blurred? Or suppose that the income source is not clearly one or the other: What part of a small shopkeeper's income derives from her labor, her capital, and her location? Most likely, she does not know. In the real world, the theoretical groups of workers, capitalists, and landlords can be quite hard to distinguish among real people.

A different approach is to use groups that are observed on the basis of *observed membership*—to use the categories that are most important to the people who have to live with them. In this way, meaningful group differences and categorical inequalities can be diagnosed and analyzed.

How Do Social Categories Arise and Evolve?

Categorical inequalities arise because humans are social animals. We form groups, at the beginning as an extension of our families: clans, tribes, nations. These groups are mutual-protection societies; insiders enjoy privileges from which outsiders are excluded. At each level, the group holds territory and its members enjoy access—sometimes exclusive—to the living and the wealth available from that land. Families, clans, tribes, and nations are also instruments of social organization and competition for available resources. Some are more powerful, numerous, and wealthy; others less so. Groups extract loyalty from their members because of the preferred status they confer, and this is true even of disadvantaged groups. Almost no matter how poor a family, clan, tribe, or nation, it is better to be a member of one, rather than to be cast out and on one's own.

Groups of this primordial type are often *patrilineal*, meaning that membership passes from the father, or sometimes *matrilineal*, from the mother. That also means that membership can be changed, by the simple act of marrying out. Women typically do marry out from their families, which fact is signified by the custom of changing one's name on marriage. Either gender can marry out of a larger group, such as a tribe. In colonial America more than a few white settlers married into Native American tribes, and vice versa, though the tribes were more accepting of white men than white society was of Native American men. In the modern world, men and women alike marry into other nationalities—in most countries it remains the easiest way for a foreigner to acquire citizenship, and of course the path of such migration is predominantly from poorer nations to richer ones. However, while small groups like families are constantly being formed and broken, larger ones like nations usually lose or gain only a tiny fraction of their populations from the outside in any given year.

As human societies developed and interacted, the structure of group memberships became more complex. Entire classes of association came into being, and each individual would come to be represented by a spectrum of identifications. *Social class* in some societies has been very well defined: landed aristocracy, merchants or bourgeoisie, working classes or proletariat. *Caste* is another complex structure with a long history in Hindu India. In modern China, something similar occurs as a result of the accident of birth: those from the rural areas have limited legal rights when they come to the cities. *Political parties* have been an important grouping structure; as Gilbert and Sullivan noted,

> That every boy and every gal
> That's born into the world alive
> Is either a little Liberal,
> Or else a little Conservative.

Today, in the United States, political parties are no longer mass organizations—but your college alumni association may be.

One group structure of great importance was religion, which was (and sometimes still is) literally a matter of life and death—massively in the case of mid-twentieth century European Jews, attacked by the Nazis, poignantly in the recent instance of the Yazidis in Northern Iraq, attacked by the Islamic State. The terms *heathen, pagan, infidel* speak to the special savagery with which religious insiders have in past times looked upon outsiders, and sometimes still do.

Religion, like marriage, is an exclusive category. You can belong to only one at any given time; while changing is possible, it involves elaborate rites of education and initiation. In some cases, the differences between groups are inconsequential—is there a significant gap between the incomes of Methodists and Lutherans, for instance? In other cases, religious identity is a fundamental determinant of personal income and economic well-being, thanks to some prior history of privilege and exclusion. This at one point was true of the basic division in American society between Protestants, Catholics, and Jews—but it is likely that that difference is less now than it once was.

Other examples of near-exclusive categories include your college fraternity or sorority, your college alumni association, your primary professional identification (or guild), and membership in the Cosa Nostra. Some of these matter a great deal to economic standing—they were created to be vehicles of exclusivity and privilege. Nationality is almost equally exclusive; a few people these days have multiple passports, but this is a recent development and the numbers are very small.

Then there are categories that are fluid, and within which you can belong to several groups at the same time. Ancestry is a good example; most people in modern America and elsewhere can identify themselves as having roots in many different communities, each of which is self-defined in its own ways. (This author has four children, whose ancestries are Scottish, English, German, French, Yankee, Southern, Canadian, Cherokee, and Chinese.) And ancestry is closely linked to *race*, but it is not quite the same thing. Race—though ostensibly ancestral—is not generally considered to be pluralistic, in the way that ancestry generally is.

Surely *race*, of all the sources of categorical inequality, is one of the most important, and one of the strangest.

What Is Race and Why Does It Matter?

One way to begin to explore the vexed topic of race in America is to note that, at time of writing, the race of the President of the United States was "African American." What does that mean?

The term *African American* serves, in the United States, as a racial category. It is so referred to, for example, on Census forms, which allow *Black* and *Negro* to serve as synonyms. In common language, African American typically refers to a group of people, *some* of whose ancestors have lived in the Western Hemisphere for centuries, having originally been brought from the African continent involuntarily as slaves. Very few African Americans descend exclusively from slaves, but the common core of the group is such descent. It is an ancestral but also a social definition: the bond is that link to slavery. It is also not a matter of kinship in any sense, since African slaves came from many different and distinct tribal and language groups.

How does President Barack Obama fit into that definition? It is a curious fact that while President Obama is undoubtedly African American, he fits the common definition not at all. His biological father, Barack Obama Sr., was a Kenyan, of the Luo tribal group, which (being in East Africa) was remote from the slaving regions that supplied the Americas. Obama Sr. was not American; he resided for a time in the United States but eventually returned to live and work in Kenya. The President's mother, Ann Dunham, was white. President Obama himself was raised in a white household.

So when did young Barry Obama emerge as an African American? It is true that he was assigned that identity on his birth certificate, by a doctor. But it appears that he became part of the African American community for the first time as a young adult, in college, and then as a community organizer in south Chicago. In some sense, he became African American as a matter of choice. Something similar can be said of Colin Powell, the former Secretary of State, whose family origins are in Jamaica. Had Secretary Powell stayed on in Jamaica, he would not have been African American. He would have been, simply, Jamaican.

These cases are atypical, but they point to an inescapable generalization about the nature of "race." Race is not a biological designation. It is a social definition, peculiar to the customs, laws, and habits of particular countries. The "race" of African Americans is a powerful source of the personal identity of many Americans. But it is a social grouping, not a biological one, which exists only in the United States of America and nowhere else.

In recent past times, the lines demarcating racial groups were reinforced by legal definitions, which were applied (and could vary) by individual states. For instance, in the state of Louisiana and elsewhere in the South, the "one drop of blood" rule applied. This stated that if one had any ancestor, however remote, who originated in Africa, then one was "Negro" or "black" in the eyes of the laws of that state. The law was enacted, of course, for the purpose of isolating a small group of allegedly unmixed whites, and giving them preferential access to civil and political rights and public services. This peculiar definition turned many Louisianans of pale hue into "blacks," and the resulting discrimination prompted some of those to attempt to "pass" as whites. Happily, those legal definitions are now extinct; today one can answer the "race" question on the census form however one pleases.

In South Africa, until the liberation of 1994, the legal system of apartheid created a three-class state: black, white, and colored—this last category included a substantial Asian Indian population. (The Japanese were regarded as "honorary whites.") It was a regime of strict privilege and enforced membership, extending to prohibition of marriage and fornication across racial lines. In other societies, racial identification is intended to protect the identity and group integrity of vulnerable minorities; this was the case (as a matter of rhetoric, at least) for "national minorities" in the former Soviet Union and in modern China, as well as for indigenous and aboriginal peoples in Brazil, Canada, and Australia, among other countries. In practice, the separate status of such groups can be an instrument for repression, as the experience of Native Americans of the United States—to begin with—makes clear.

It should be obvious that in a social grouping, with deeply diverse and mixed ancestries, discussions of *inherited* group characteristics are illogical. This has not stopped many racist psuedoscientists from publishing treatises showing the inferiority of one group or the superiority of another.

Race is a problematic category, and there are countries that do not recognize racial classification at all. France is an example. However, that does not mean that race is an unimportant social marker in France; there, as almost everywhere, the appearance of racial identity remains a strong categorizing force. And that perception, in turn, plays an important role in creating insider-outsider relationships, which form the underpinning of social and spatial segregation and discriminatory practices in education, employment, and professional advancement. These practices, and the economic inequalities that they spawn and reinforce, form the central challenge that the odd categorical inequality we call "race" poses for a modern state and society. Without doubt, they will remain so, as long as the goals of equality and justice remain both important and elusive.

Why Is Gender Inequality Important?

The greatest distinction in all animal species is that between male and female, in humans between man and woman. Unlike race, it is a distinction with a clear biological basis, though that distinction is effaced in a certain number of cases by transgender individuals. For this and other reasons, it is useful to distinguish between *sex* and *gender* and to specify that the word *gender* is not a biological term, but a matter of social presentation.

Inequalities between men and women are pervasive. Women work harder, have lower status, and are paid less, almost everywhere. In working- and middle-class families, they also do a high share of the errands, the housework, the child care, and the caring for older people in the home. The major exceptions are those who marry and form the unemployed part of a high-income household, and whose lives may then be taken up with administering and managing the consumption activities of that household, including directing the work of household staff—usually female.

In economic terms, it is difficult to say that women as a group are worse off than men, because so many women and men form common households and so enjoy a common living standard and equal or near-equal access to the household wealth. But in the United States women who are employed earn, on average, about 77 cents for every dollar earned by their male counterparts—although a significant part of that differential is accounted for, in statistical terms, by differences in observed characteristics (such as age and education) other than gender. Women still tend to be channeled into "feminized" professions, such as teaching or nursing, which have relatively low pay and status in relation to the education required to enter them. Some professions (such as the civil service) have become more feminized over time as they have lost relative economic status. And while formal barriers to the "higher" professions and to the top levels of the corporate world have been lowered over the past generation in the United States, the proportion of women who make it to the very top in finance, or industry, or government, or tenured university appointments, remains low.

Meanwhile—as Marx already observed—the automation of manufacturing and the growth of the services sector has opened large numbers of low-status jobs to women, not only in the United States but around the world; a major part of the Chinese manufacturing labor force consists of young rural women; the same is true in sweatshops the world over. In America, working women who find themselves at the head of young families are much more likely to be poor, or near poverty, than single working men. Divorce, notoriously, causes women's income to fall while the income and living standard of the departing male partner tends to rise. Elderly single women, who often have not enjoyed high earnings when they were younger, tend to be at the bottom of the living scales for elderly people.

Decidedly, the liberation of women has been, and still is, one of the most challenging and difficult social and economic causes of all time.

What Are Nationality and Legal Status, and Why Do They Matter?

In economic terms, perhaps the most important socio-legal category of them all is one that we often don't think that much about: *nationality* and legal status. This one refers to a clear-cut, near-universal, almost exclusive attribute of every human being on earth: Which country do they belong to, and in which country do they have the right to reside?

The nation-state is a fundamental categorical unit. Only the high seas and Antarctica, where almost no one lives, are free of control by some nation-state. Nationality is the attribute of citizenship, into which almost every human being is born. Nationality conveys a right to live in the country to which one belongs—but it also implies that one may be excluded, or treated as a political and economic inferior—in any other country. Since the differences of average income and living standards across the countries of the earth can be very large, nationality is the most important correlate of economic wealth and well-being. People who live in rich countries tend to be rich by world standards; for instance, there are almost no Germans who fall below the world median income. People who live in very poor countries are for the most part very poor. There may be a few rich among them—the great landlords, mining barons, and kleptocrats—but if the population at large were not poor, the country could not be poor.

Here an important distinction should be drawn. What do we mean when we say a nation is poor? There are two ways of measuring this. One is to ask about how people live; how much they can consume, how long their lives may be; what access they have to free time and amenities. This involves comparing physical consumption inside the region; economists call this comparison on a basis of "purchasing power parity." The other is to compare the purchasing power of money incomes in the world marketplace—what your income can buy if you happen to go someplace else. This depends on exchange rates, and here the citizens of rich countries have a big advantage; their money incomes are often worth a lot more in poor countries than they are at home. Conversely, most citizens of poor countries would have a hard time moving to rich countries without finding a rich-country source of income. Nationality is therefore economic destiny, for the most part.

But not entirely. Where great inequalities exist across national lines, some people do move. Migration and immigration are driven by economic inequality. If a citizen of a poor country moves to a rich country and finds a job—even a hard and bad job—it is likely that they will earn much more, in cash-value terms, than they ever could at home. That's why they come! The living conditions in the new country may be harsh, even nearly unbearable. But a fraction of the new income can be sent home, where it can be converted into the poor-country's money and where it will go a long way.

Rich countries therefore attract many immigrants from less-favored places—and especially in recent times, which has been hard on poor-country development but good for facilitating travel. The rich countries must then face the question of what to do about the immigrants. As the immigrant population grows—especially if the people involved are present illegally and do not have the formal right to live and work in their new country—there also grows an underclass of second-class residents with no political voice and few civil rights. Their presence makes it easier to undermine working conditions for native workers, or simply to render them unemployed, since it is possible (and profitable) to design jobs that immigrants will accept but that natives would not. So the choice is between mass deportations—a moral and humanitarian catastrophe—and the extension of political rights, which seems only fair except to those who fear that it will open the floodgates for more immigrants to arrive. It's a dilemma that so far no country has effectively resolved, which is why immigration remains a hot political issue, even in a "country of immigrants" like the United States.

Can Categorical Inequalities Be Eliminated?

The short answer to this question is, no. Categorical inequalities exist in all societies, and they will never disappear entirely. But they do sometimes change in character over time. It's possible for a particular stigmatized population to become, with time by dint of special effort, "mainstream" and to lose its character of "disadvantaged." This has been true, in the United States, of numerous ethnic communities of European origin, including Irish, Italians, and Jews. In recent years many disadvantages associated with physical disability have been overcome, thanks to the Americans with Disabilities Act. The stigmatization associated with unorthodox sexual orientation and gender identity has also declined.

Even so, it remains the case that to be black as opposed to white in America implies, on average, a significant gap in income and a massive shortfall in personal wealth; African American families are much more likely to clock in at net financial wealth of zero than other groups. And where black America has moved up the income scale—largely by abandoning, over the years, the hard life of southern farm work—a new underclass has moved in to take its place. These are the undocumented migrants of Mexican and Central American origin, whose place at the bottom of the ladder is cemented by low wages, Spanish language, transient employment, and unstable legal status, including a complete lack of political rights and representation.

The severity of any particular categorical inequality depends on two factors. One is the place of a particular group in the income and wealth structure—its relative position. The other is the shape of that structure in the society as a whole. Are income and wealth highly concentrated among a privileged few? Or is the society broadly egalitarian, with modest gaps from low to high, and effective social insurance and other protections for the most vulnerable? In the latter case, while invidious distinctions and discrimination remain a problem, the cost of that problem is much less than it otherwise would be.

If Not, How Should They Be Approached?

These reflections and long experience suggest that there are two approaches to reducing the severity of categorical inequalities. One is to focus on the position of groups. The other is to focus on the structure of pay, incomes, and wealth.

Policies that focus on the position of groups include civil rights laws, voting rights laws, housing and school integration, affirmative action, and immigration reform. Since these policies run hard against the prevailing biases and attitudes of society, they inevitably run into fierce opposition. In some cases, as with affirmative action, they may in the end serve purposes not as pure as originally intended; it's a fair characterization that affirmative action in today's high-end college admissions is mainly a form of competition to attract the talented and well-prepared children of the African American and Hispanic middle classes. This is not a bad thing, since great schools need a diverse student body, and minority communities need highly qualified professionals, leaders, and exemplars. But affirmative action practiced this way rarely serves to open doors to the truly disadvantaged.

Policies that focus on the structure of pay, income, and wealth include minimum wages, collective bargaining rights, Social Security, universal health insurance, unemployment insurance, financial regulation, progressive income taxation, and the taxation of estates and gifts. Measures of this type ease the stress associated with being near the bottom of the income and wealth structure, and so increase the mobility of individuals as they strive to climb the ladder. Both types of policy have an important place in any struggle for a better, fairer, and more just national society. But neither type addresses the greatest categorical inequality of all, which is the gulf between nations in the world.

4

MAJOR CONCEPTS OF DISTRIBUTION

As you have probably noticed, *economic inequality* is a term covering a great many distinct ideas and concepts and measures. Here we will introduce the major terms that have operational meaning, because governments (and others) tend to collect data on them, and so they will be used later on. We will try to make the experience not too painful.

What Is Income?

Income is the most commonly measured metric of economic success and status, and the distribution of income is the most widely known and used metric of inequality. But income comes in multiple forms, so it is important to be careful to specify exactly what one means.

In countries with income tax, income means (exactly) what the tax authorities determine it to mean. The tax authorities will tell you what you must include and what you may exclude. For instance, in the United States, business expenses and charitable contributions may be deducted from your income, before you report (and pay tax) on the remainder. The thinking is that business income should be counted net of expenses, since it takes money to earn money, and that when you contribute to a church or other tax-exempt entity, you are passing along income rather than keeping it for yourself.

The result is that countries with well-enforced income taxes have a very good idea of what their taxpayers earn as income—but that idea will not be the same as for other countries with different tax codes, or across time when tax laws change. In the United States in 1986, for instance, a Tax Reform Act abolished many deductions and exemptions for high-income people, and then taxed the larger amounts that were reported at a lower rate. Naturally the income reported by high-income people went up, and this has been a source of confusion in the income-distribution statistics ever since.

Many countries do not have income tax and therefore do not have tax records for income. In such countries, the principal means of learning about income is to take surveys (as the United States and other countries with income taxes also do). Surveys must specify what counts as income, and they typically allow respondents to specify their income as falling within a range: zero to ten thousand, ten to twenty, and so forth. In poor countries this question can be complicated by the question of whether to measure *in-kind* income—income earned but not in monetary form. If you are a merchant in a village of goat-herds, and someone pays you with a goat, how should that count in your measure of income?

Income is typically earned by a person, and the distribution of income across persons is called, unsurprisingly, the *personal distribution of income*. The degree of inequality in the personal distribution is a useful measure of economic structure; it tells us whether jobs (and hours) are paid in a relatively egalitarian or deeply unequal way. But it is not a suitable measure of the inequality of economic welfare, because most people do not organize their consuming lives as separate individuals. Rather they live in households, some with multiple earners and some with only one or none at all. And households pool their incomes in order to better manage their consumption.

The *household distribution of income* is a basic measure of the equality of access to economic resources. It tells us whether the means of life are evenly or unevenly spread. But again there are complications. Households may be large or small, and their living standards, for a given income, will be lower if they are large and higher if they are small. Economists use *equivalence scales* to try to adjust for this difficulty.

If the cost of living is different in different parts of a country, another issue arises. Should one adjust for the fact that it is cheaper to live in the country than in town? If you do, you will have a measure of *real income* and of the equality or inequality of the real income distribution. But then you may lose sight of the fact that many people prefer the high money incomes of the big city, even if it is much more expensive to live there. Why? Because big cities have many public goods and services (culture, entertainment, social life) for which they do not charge directly, and because cash earned in the big city may be spent elsewhere, getting the best of both worlds.

Such complications tell us that even the "simple" concept of income is fraught with measurement difficulties and ambiguities of concept. But we are only at the beginning.

In measuring the inequality of personal or household income, it is important to specify what type or concept of income is referred to, since different concepts will typically yield sharply differing results. Three important income concepts are market income, gross income, and net or disposable income.

What Is Market Income?

Market income refers to cash income earned by individual economic activity. It includes wages and salaries (income from work), and it includes dividends, interest, stock option realizations, and realized capital gains (income from capital). It includes rent, which is income from the ownership of land. Market income excludes public pensions, unemployment insurance, and other subsidies and benefits that do not arise from "market" activities. The concept is considered useful by those who feel it is important to distinguish between income flowing from the economy and income flowing from the state.

A paradox of advanced social democracies is that market income in them is usually very unequal—much more unequal than any other type of income. Part of this is due to the fact that in all capitalist countries—social democratic or otherwise—the ownership of capital assets and high-value land is concentrated in a very few hands, that these yield the highest incomes, and that advanced social democracies are generally quite competent at requiring and enforcing record-keeping for tax and other purposes. Meanwhile, most working households hold few income-producing assets; they rely wholly or almost wholly on labor income.

But a larger part of the paradox stems from the fact that advanced social democracies have many households with no market income. This is because the formation of households is not independent of the structure of incomes. Advanced social democracies have generous welfare states, and so their retired elderly, single parents, and others can often afford to live in independent households. So they tend to do so, often migrating to and congregating in low-cost areas, whether in the north of Denmark or the south of Texas. In countries without strong public pensions and child support, people without market income are obliged to live in households with people who have some. As a result, the inequality of market income may not be so high, although the inequality of household income as a whole may be higher.

What Is Gross Income?

Gross income refers to all flows of money income, whether from market or non-market sources. It includes especially public pensions and other benefits from "transfer programs." It would exclude only such things as income required to cover business expenses and other items that can normally be excluded from taxable income. It does not exclude that part of income which is paid as taxes.

The concept of gross income inequality is useful for assessing the degree of egalitarianism in the social and economic structure of any country. In empirical studies, rankings of gross income inequality correspond most closely to what most people regard as the common sense of the matter. That is, the social democracies of northern Europe rank lowest, along with the formerly communist states of Eastern Europe, which had highly compact wage distributions and no income from capital ownership. Capitalist welfare states in Southern Europe and North America show higher inequality, but this is still low on the scale when compared to the tropical and less-developed world. Fundamentally, the measure of gross household income inequality appears to capture quite well the predominance, weakness, or absence of a robust industrial and post-industrial middle class.

Gross income is, however, also not a measure of economic welfare. What you have available to spend is a matter of *net* income, after the government collects its direct taxes.

What Is Net or Disposable Income?

Net or disposable income is what is left over after receiving all market and non-market incomes, and after paying the direct taxes that are due on those incomes, and not including payments that are immediately deducted for health insurance, retirement, and other purposes. Here, finally, is a measure of what the household has available to spend.

Household net income, after adjusting for household size, and ignoring differences in the cost of living, is a more or less accurate measure of *current* economic welfare. Households that have more disposable income are (widely thought to be) better off, and conversely. This is not true of market income, and it may or may not be true, depending on taxes, of gross income.

In the advanced countries, the distribution of household net income is far more egalitarian than the distribution of gross income or market income. That is because taxes—at least income and capital gains taxes—are progressive in their effects, meaning that they take a higher proportion from the rich than from the poor. (Also, wealthier people may defer and shelter more of their income, and pay for more expensive forms of insurance.) The income tax is overtly progressive; it has a rising scale of marginal rates. But other taxes, such as the tax on capital gains or common stock dividends, are also paid almost exclusively by the rich. And the effect is progressive, even if the tax rate on these types of income is lower than the tax rate on ordinary income. The reason is that the bottom 90 percent of income earners have very few capital gains or dividends to tax; hence the burden of that tax rate does not fall on them.

However, net income is counted before people pay the most regressive taxes, which are the taxes on consumption, such as sales taxes, or the Value-Added-Tax in Europe. Since poor people consume a higher fraction of their incomes (and in local shops) than rich people, the burden of sales taxes falls disproportionately on those with less income. There are, however, no data that adjust the distribution of household well-being for the effect of consumption taxes; net income is the most pared-down income concept that we have.

In countries without advanced welfare states, there is little to no difference between measured inequalities of market, gross, and net income. These countries fall into two types: the less-developed nations, where all types of inequality are quite high; and some of the post-communist states of Eastern Europe, where all types remain quite low. In the Eastern European states, the legacy of egalitarian communist wage structures appears not to have yet been wholly erased; the collapse of communism, however, did bring on (at least at first) a decline of social services, including public health services, education, and culture, that were a mainstay of life under the old regimes. The result is a society that is broadly egalitarian still, but with little effective redistribution and weak public services.

With all of these complications, getting good comparative measures of inequality across countries and through time is a challenge. Several attempts have been made to meet that challenge, notably by the Luxembourg Income Study and by the University of Texas Inequality Project, each using very different approaches and techniques. We will return to this problem.

With good modern data sets on the actual dispersion of income, earnings, or pay across nations, it is possible to study the statistical properties of the distribution taken as a whole. The sub-branch of *econophysics* has taken up this challenge, showing how in practice national income distributions tend to follow one particular pattern for the bottom 95 percent or so (a log-normal distribution, which is statistically the distribution most likely to appear in such a situation). Meanwhile, for the top 5 percent or so, a different distribution called a power law appears, which accounts for the numbers of people found in successively higher income brackets.

What Is the Distribution of Income across Nations?

Yet another categorical approach to the distribution of income is to use the nation-state as the category of interest. That is, one may wish to compute the inequality of income measured between countries, where one has only the population and the average income of each country, measured in terms of purchasing power parities, or the internal living standard that income in that country will bring.

The former World Bank economist Branko Milanovic distinguishes two concepts of the distribution of income between countries. Concept I, as he calls it, is a simple measure of the variation of incomes between countries, unweighted by population. This has the disadvantage of treating China and (say) Barbados as having equal importance. Concept II weights each country by its population—which has the disadvantage of giving 40 percent of the world weight to China and India alone.

These two approaches give diverging results for the late twentieth century. Concept I shows rising inequality between countries, especially from 1980 to 2000. Concept II shows a decline, because the purchasing power parity (PPP) measures of income in China (at least, those in use at the time) show a very sharp increase in well-being in that country, moving the Chinese population from the bottom of the scale into the lower middle class. But of course, China is a big country, and it is possible to divide it up in various ways, say by measuring urban and rural incomes separately. If you do that, then Concept II inequality no longer shows a decline, since a large part of the Chinese rural population was not so strongly affected by the country's rising average income. Truly there is no single best solution!

What Is the Global Income Distribution?

A final way to study the income distribution is to attempt to measure the inequality of incomes of the population of the whole world; Milanovic calls this Concept III inequality. The idea is to treat each person (or household) on an equal basis, and to assess where each stands in relationship to all the others, on the principle of common membership in the human species. The method is to merge household surveys taken all around the world, and to convert the income of each household to a common currency unit, using purchasing power parity measures of the relative value of each currency.

Empirical results for this exercise are limited, since data on the scale required have been collected only fairly recently for a large enough sample of countries, including China and India, who contribute some 40 percent of the persons and households to such an estimate. Moreover, blending the diverse household surveys requires access to an archive of such surveys, and of course a good deal of very careful comparison. In the most recent work, estimates were available for only four separate years, beginning only in the late 1980s.

The results show that nationality predominates in the distribution of global income. If a country is counted as poor on average, almost all of its citizens will be counted as having incomes below the world median, irrespective of where they stand in the internal distribution. If a country is rich, almost all of its citizens will have incomes in the top half, and most of them will be in the top quarter of world incomes. At the global scale, where you stand in the distribution of a small country counts for much less than where your country stands in the world.

But this also means that the estimates depend heavily on the accuracy of PPP measurements across countries. And this is a problem, because people in different countries do not generally consume the same basket of consumption goods. Households in China, for instance, consume very little of a number of Western staples (such as fresh milk) and of Western luxuries (such as Scotch whiskey). If one includes these items at their weight in Western consumption, China seems a very expensive place to live. The distortion arises because there is no certainty that Chinese households will ever develop a strong taste for such products as their incomes rise; it is therefore illusory to think of such households as poor merely because they cannot afford what they do not want.

Has the global distribution of incomes changed? Not by very much, so far as we can tell. In broad terms, the rise in inequality within most countries is offset, globally, by the rise of a large Chinese middle class, bringing many millions out of extreme poverty. The calculation of a global income distribution is an interesting exercise, but some scholars remain doubtful of its relevance to any actual economic issue. After all, policies are still determined largely by nation-states or by trading blocs (the case of Europe). To the extent that policies ever address inequality as a problem, they will do so within the limits of their reach and jurisdiction, which does not extend to the entire planet.

What Is the Distribution of Expenditure?

In a number of countries, especially in Asia, economists have chosen (for the most part) not to attempt to survey incomes, but to look instead at the consumption or expenditure patterns of households and to survey those instead. This approach is especially useful for countries where a large part of the population grows its own food, or barters personal service for food and shelter, which would not normally be counted in a survey of cash income. On the other hand, a focus on consumption also means that the savings of the wealthy are not counted, so a substantial part of cash income escapes the survey-taker. For both reasons, consumption or expenditure inequality is almost always far lower than income inequality, of any type, but especially lower than gross or market inequality, when both are measured in the same society.

To take an example, consumption-based surveys in India for many years showed that country as being relatively egalitarian, if the inequality measure for India were simply compared to (say) those for major Latin American countries, where income surveys have been the rule. However, recent efforts to measure income inequality in India show that society to be highly unequal, indeed among the most unequal in the world. The income data are consistent with the extremes of wealth and poverty that one observes.

What Is Pay and What Is the Distribution of Pay?

A final concept in our panorama is that of *pay*. Whereas income and expenditure are measured at the level of individuals and households, and refer to the inflow and outflow of resources to those units, pay is a concept that is attached not to a person but to a *job*. It is what the employer shells out, for a certain quantity of time worked. A job may be held, over time, by several different people. People and households may (and often do) hold more than one job. There is thus no direct translation from the inequality on the employer's side of the ledger to that on the household's side; a large household holding just one well-paid job may be relatively stretched, while a small one holding three or four modest jobs could be quite well-off, at least in money terms.

The advantage of data on pay is that it is easily available, over many countries and many years. Household records are decentralized if they exist at all; except where there are good tax systems, collecting them requires taking surveys, which is expensive. Households come and go, so tracking them through time is tricky, although in the United States the Panel Survey on Income Dynamics (PSID) exists to do exactly that. And in countries where surveys were not taken in the past, they cannot be reconstructed after the fact; you cannot go asking households what their income was twenty or thirty years ago. Employers, on the other hand, tend to persist, and because they are businesses, they keep books. So finding payroll records is relatively easy. Moreover, instead of taking a sample, one can have the entire universe of this information fairly readily at hand. Businesses above a certain size are required, in most countries, to report their employment and payrolls, so national governments collect this type of information routinely, and store it over long periods of time.

What Is the Sectoral or Regional Distribution of Pay?

The difficulty of raw pay data is that it is often not readily available, because governments have an obligation to maintain the privacy of individual respondents, and in the case of big businesses, very often the dominant employer in some town or region, they would be all too easy to identify in many cases. But it is often not necessary to work with the original data sources. What governments routinely publish is, very often, quite good enough for measuring the major trends in inequalities of pay. These are tables of employment and payrolls by sector and region.

Sectoral data of this type are typically collected by national governments according to some favored national classification scheme; a typical simple case might divide up payrolls into agriculture, industry, finance, construction, services, forestry and fisheries, and a few other distinct categories. As we shall see later, even a relatively crude decomposition of this type can be used to construct a crude, but effective, measure of the inequality of pay across the sectors. And if the classification scheme becomes more precise, for instance by subdividing industry into a plethora of distinct subtypes, then the measure of inequality becomes more precise as well.

Regional inequalities can be calculated in the same way, by taking advantage of the fact that all countries collect data from their provinces or states, and the provinces collect them from counties, the counties from towns, and so forth, all the way down. Where subnational regions collect data by sectors, one can measure inequalities across sectors within regions, allowing both the type of activity and the location to vary. In this way, it is possible to construct very detailed, very precise pictures of how relative pay has been distributed and how the distributions have changed through time.

For some analytical purposes, income is the desired measure—for example, if one is interested in capturing differences in household well-being. For other purposes, pay is a better measure. For example, economic theory has long focused on the determination of the hourly wage, although hourly wage *rates* are almost never measured directly (and in some jobs, like farming, they do not exist). But payroll data come closer to the concept of the hourly wage than data based on incomes do, since the latter are typically collected as weekly earnings, which depend on hours worked, and in which jobs. Pay is a direct measure of cash outlay by the business for a certain number of hours.

It turns out, moreover, that variations of relative pay or income across major sectors, or between major economic regions within countries, can account for a surprisingly large share of the variations in the economy as a whole. Much of China's increasing inequality, for example, is due to the rise of its coastal cities, and within China's provinces, much is due to the rise of finance, transport, utilities, and other sectors with monopoly power. Much of the rise in inequality in the United States in the late 1990s was due to incomes booked in just five counties: Manhattan, three counties of Silicon Valley, California, and King County, Washington—home of Microsoft. From a sectoral standpoint, this was the rise of finance and technology and almost nothing else.

How close are measures of inequality constructed from pay to measures constructed from income? The answer in most cases is: surprisingly close. And that discovery permits us to construct statistical models linking the two approaches. We can take advantage of the great availability of pay data, in order to estimate measures of income inequality, which are of greater interest to economists who are attempting to study the distribution of economic well-being.

Conclusion

This chapter has taken a sweeping tour of concepts of income, expenditure, and pay that underpin the study of economic inequality in most cases. The chapter is here to underpin the fact that when working on inequality, one must always know exactly what it is that is being measured. Otherwise, the measurements will not end up meaning very much.

We shall take up the inequality of wealth at a later point.

5

MEASURES OF INEQUALITY

In this short chapter, we take up another fairly technical topic: How can inequality be measured? We will not attempt to give a full technical treatment of this question, but will introduce the reader to some of the most commonly used concepts and techniques, and we hope in accessible language.

What Is a Distribution?

In very simple terms, a distribution is a plot that puts income, expenditure, pay, or wealth on the horizontal, and the number of people at each level of the x-variable on the vertical axis. In the cases of income, expenditure, or pay, the distribution starts at zero since there is no such thing as a negative value of these variables.

Measures of inequality concern the *shape* of the distribution of income, or wealth, or pay. Typically the unit of observation in the distribution is the individual, or the household. If you think of a diagram with income levels on the x-axis and on the y-axis the numbers of people or households at each level, the usual shape of the distribution is to rise sharply from a very low value, to peak at the modal income (that level enjoyed, or not enjoyed, by the largest group of people), and then to tail off to the right. Usually the distribution will have a very long tail, reflecting small numbers of people or households with very high income. If society becomes more equal, the part in the middle becomes taller, and the tail flattens out. If society becomes less equal, then the hump in the middle becomes flatter and the tail tends to become a bit fat. Changes in this shape are subject to statistical measurement.

It is possible to fit mathematical functions to the distribution of income, and the usual result resembles a *log-normal* distribution, meaning that the logarithms of the income values follow a bell curve or Gaussian or normal distribution (see Figure 5.1). Closer examination of actual distributions suggest that in reality they are (a bit) better modeled by thinking of them as a blend of two distributions. For the bottom 95 percent or so, the best fit is a log-linear distribution. For those at the

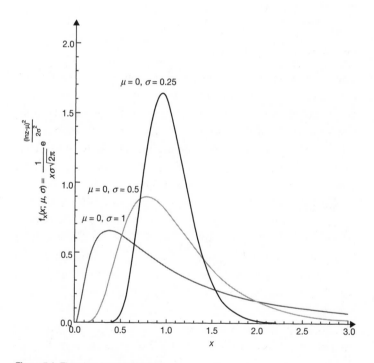

Figure 5.1 Three Log-Normal Distributions

The tall distribution in red is the most equal; that which peaks on the left is the least equal. Note the tails.

very top, the better fit is a Pareto distribution or a power law, which states that the proportion of people with an income above a certain value is a function (for example, a square root) of that value.

A consequence of having a power law distribution at the top is that income may be very unequally shared; there will be more ultra-rich than there would be under a log-normal distribution. (This is known as having a "fat tail.") A power law is the mathematical form underlying the common 80–20 rule, which in its original formulation was the discovery (by Vilfredo Pareto) that 20 percent of Italians held 80 percent of Italian land. Many other variations of this principle have since been proposed, suggesting that power laws are quite common in the real world.

What Is the Range and What Is the Inter-Quartile Range?

The *range* is the simplest possible indicator of a distribution. For income it is the distance, measured in currency units, between the highest and the lowest value in the sample under observation. Simple as that—but not very informative. The low and the high values may be anomalies, far removed from most of the other observations. So to know the range is not to know very much about the population.

The *inter-quartile range* is a way of lopping off the extreme values, in order to look at only the middle part of a distribution, where the "middle 50 percent" of the observations lie. The inter-quartile range is calculated by lining up all the observations in order of income, and then removing both the top and bottom 25 percent. The range for the remainder is the inter-quartile range.

The inter-quartile range conveys some information about the center of the distribution, but not very much. And like the full range, it is measured in the original unit of observation (dollars), so it's very hard to compare to other range measures in other currencies or at different times, when the value of the dollar unit was different from what it is today.

What Are Quantiles and What Are Quantile Ratios?

These simple observations tell us that to measure inequality in a meaningful way, we need a way to do so that is not dependent on the currency unit, which therefore can be compared across space, time, and countries in a consistent manner.

One simple way to do this is again to line up all the observations from low to high, and to count them off in percentage terms, point by point. The resulting groups are called *percentiles*. If instead you count by 10-percent groups, you have *deciles*. If you group in bunches of 20 percent of the population each, you have a standard category known as *a quintile*. Each of these is an instance of a general practice known as taking *quantiles*. (Quintiles, quantiles, let's call the whole thing off.)

A *quantile ratio* is the income level at some particular percentile, divided by the income level at some other percentile. Quantile ratios are commonly known by the two percentiles they involve: thus the 90–10 ratio is the ratio of income at the 90th percentile to income at the 10th percentile. Taking this ratio can be a useful quick-and-dirty way of gauging the changing inequality of a distribution through time, without the potential distortion of a few extreme cases. Similarly, the 90–50 ratio may be taken as an index of inequality among the upper-middle classes, while the 50–10 ratio suggests the extent of relative deprivation at the lower end of the scale. The 75–25 ratio is the inter-quartile ratio, not to be confused with the inter-quartile *range*.

These measures are each useful, and they are unit-free, which means that different distributions can now be compared. But notice that they involve only two pieces of information: the income levels at each of two separated percentiles. All the other information from the underlying distribution—which must be collected in order to compute percentiles in the first place—is simply thrown away.

What Is the Palma Ratio?

The *Palma ratio* is the recent invention of Cambridge University economist Gabriel Palma. It consists of the ratio of the income share of the top decile to that of the bottom two quintiles. The intuition behind choosing this ratio is that the excluded upper-middle, from the third quintile through the ninth decile, seems (according to Palma's research) to maintain a fairly stable share of total income in many countries. Thus changing inequality is substantially a shift from the poorest 40 percent to the top 10 percent, or vice versa.

The Palma ratio is designed to be a simple and sensitive measure of such shifts, and it is enjoying a certain popularity as this is written. Whether it will go on to become a standard summary measure of inequalities remains to be seen. A limitation lies in the fact that in order to calculate it, you must first have income measures from a survey or micro-sample, from which one can measure the deciles of the income distribution. This is a limitation of all percentile-based inequality measures, and also of the Gini coefficient, to which we will turn shortly.

What Are the Top Shares and What Do We Know about Them?

A difficulty of survey-based measures of income inequality is the practice of "top-coding." Usually in administering a survey one cannot ask for respondents to reveal their exact incomes. So instead the survey-taker asks respondents to enter a range within which their income falls, and the analyst later makes some assumption about how incomes are distributed within that range. (Often, the simplest assumption is that "between $50K and $60K in annual income" means $55K.)

The difficulty arises because at the very top of the income scale, it is necessary to leave an open-ended category. So the survey may have as an option, "income greater than $250K." Or, "income greater than $1m." And that leaves open the question, how much greater? While we may imagine that in a given population most people who report annual incomes over a million dollars are actually earning quite close to that sum, there may be a few earning a hundred or even a thousand times as much.

An approach to this problem is to turn to income tax records, where individuals are required to specify their exact taxable incomes. Tax records are confidential, but anonymized files permit researchers to calculate the share of total taxable income earned by small numbers of people at the very top of the distribution: the top 1 percent, the top 0.1 percent, and even the top .01 percent in some cases. This is the approach taken by Thomas Piketty, Emmanuel Saez, and Anthony Atkinson in recent research.

Yet for all their virtues, income tax records pose challenges of their own. Compared to surveys, they are not good at capturing unofficial and unreported incomes, such as cash earned in the informal sector. So the top shares may be exaggerated for that reason. Or they may be underestimated, if there is a lot of tax evasion by the very rich. More prosaically, comparing top shares across countries is problematic, because tax laws differ and therefore so do definitions of taxable income. The share of total income required to be reported for tax purposes may vary greatly between countries, even if the underlying distribution of actual cash incomes is exactly the same. Even within countries, the definition of taxable income will change when tax laws are rewritten, and this will upset the comparability of taxable-income measures over time.

Then there is the most prosaic problem, which is that one can acquire income-tax records only in countries that actually have income tax. In a recent compilation, Professor Piketty presents data for just 29 countries, not including any of the oil kingdoms of the Middle East, for instance, where it has been rumored that some of the locals are among the world's most prosperous persons.

What Are the Lorenz Curve and the Gini Coefficient?

After exploring the above simple measures, we can see that it would be nice to have a measure of inequality that is drawn from surveys, unit-free, comparable across different populations, and that makes use of all the information that a survey or census may make available about the incomes of the population under study. It should also be the case that transferring a small amount of income from a richer to a poorer person causes the index to decline. The Gini coefficient is a nice example of an inequality measure that meets these tests. It is, by far, the most popular and widely used measure of inequality in use.

The easiest way to understand the Gini coefficient is to envision the Lorenz curve, a simple plot that can be drawn for any distribution. To draw the Lorenz curve, first rank all members of the population or survey in order of income, and count them off into quintiles, deciles, or percentiles (the finer the better, for accuracy's sake). Plot the quantiles on the x-axis. On the y-axis, record the share of total income cumulatively earned up to each quantile. Thus, if the bottom 10 percent of the population earns 2 percent of the income, record a point at (10,2) and so forth. Connect the dots.

The resulting curve will be bowed below a 45-degree line, except for the case—unheard-of in real applications—of actual income equality. It will start at (0,0) and end at (100,100), since none of the people necessarily earns none of the income, and all of the people necessarily earn all of it. At any point of the curve, one can read exactly how much of total income the people below that income level have the right to call their own.

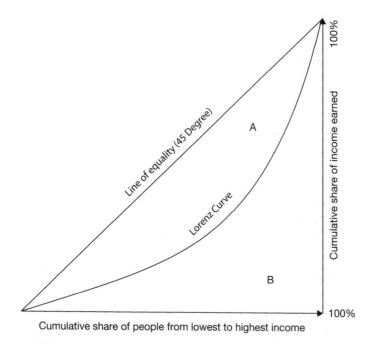

Figure 5.2 The Lorenz Curve

The Gini coefficient—invented by another Italian, Corrado Gini—is a simple geometric representation of the Lorenz curve. First, take the area between the Lorenz curve and the 45-degree line. Then divide that area by the area of the triangle below the 45-degree line—which in the case of a graph that is 100 on a side is the number 5,000. The result is the Gini coefficient. In Figure 5.2 the Gini coefficient is the ratio of the areas A and (A+B), or

$$\text{Gini} = [A / (A + B)] * 100$$

The Gini coefficient will vary from a value of zero—the case of absolute equality—to the value of 100, in the case where the last percentile holds all of the income. In income surveys of advanced countries over the past fifty years, measured Gini coefficients run from the low twenties, for such communist regimes as the German Democratic Republic, to the high sixties for some countries in sub-Saharan Africa. Measures for the major advanced countries have tended to run from the low thirties to the mid-forties, with a rising trend visible in most data sets.

Thus the Gini has the virtue of a scale that does not depend either on the unit or on the size of the population under study. You can measure it in your classroom, and compare the result to the Gini coefficient for the United States, or the entire world. You can also estimate the Gini from quintile, decile, or percentile shares, using the line segments connecting the information for these intermediate points, rather than a continuous curve. The error involved will be very small.

The Gini coefficient is very useful, fairly easy to compute, and easy to understand; no wonder it is the most popular general measure of inequality out there. But—as always!—there are limitations. The most important one is that the Gini requires a survey or a census with the underlying data; it must in principle be possible to rank the people or households from low to high and to calculate distinct quantiles of the distribution. But surveys are expensive and census records are rare; even in the United States, a census is taken only once a decade. In many countries, the historical record of income surveys is sparse, irregular, and inconsistent, and—as a result—so is the statistical record of Gini coefficients.

A subtler drawback of the Lorenz-Gini approach is that it cannot be used easily to add two populations together, or to break them apart. Suppose, for instance, that one has Gini measures for every country in Europe, alongside the average income and population of each European country. Could one compute a measure of inequality for Europe, taken as a single population? Not with any great confidence in the accuracy or reliability of the result. One cannot ever just average the Gini coefficients of two countries to get the inequality that would pertain if they were merged!

Similarly, there are many problems for which it would be useful to divide a population into constituent groups, so as to work out the inequality between the groups and the inequalities within them. It is often interesting, for instance, to do this by race or gender: to ask (for instance) how much of total inequality can be attributed to inequalities among women, among men, and between the genders? The Gini coefficient is not well suited to this calculation, even if you have underlying data that permit Gini measures for the two genders to be computed separately.

What Are Theil Statistics?

We have just one more approach to discuss. It is based on the work of a University of Chicago econometrician of the mid-twentieth century, Henri Theil (pronounced "Tile"). Theil was interested in the theory of information underlying modern computer science, and in measures of *entropy* that are developed in statistical thermodynamics, and that are closely related to the information problems of signal and noise. Theil's insight and contribution were that a measure of entropy or information content could be converted quite easily into a measure of economic inequality, and the result is a family of *Theil statistics*. One of Theil's statistics, known as *Theil's T*, is in especially common use.

The peculiar advantage of the Theil statistics is that they can be broken apart and added up. If you have two groups (say, men and women) and if you know the population and the average income of each group, then you can compute three inequality measures: inequality among women, among men, and between the two genders. The overall population inequality, computed as if you started with both genders in the same pool, will then be exactly the same as a weighted average of within-group inequalities, plus the between-group inequality. Similarly, if you have T statistics for each country in a region, and the populations and average income of each region, you can compute an inequality measure for the region as if it were one population—even if no unified survey had ever been taken.

And then there is one more advantage. Suppose (as is often the case) you don't have any survey-based evidence on incomes or expenditures at all? Suppose that all you have, for a given country or set of years, is a table, published by the government, that reports (say) payroll and employment in a classification of economic sectors, or (say) income and population by provinces, counties, and precincts? What then?

This type of data is *grouped data*. There are many different ways that groups can be defined, divided, and subdivided: by geographic boundaries, by industrial classification, by personal characteristics. Data of this type are very widely available in published form, often with quite consistent category structures, over many years for many countries. There are even international data sets at the continental and global levels that record data of this kind for industrial pay in many countries. With the Theil statistic, one can calculate a measure of inequality between groups, using whatever administrative data and group structures one may have on hand. This measure is the between-groups component of Theil's T statistic, and it has proved to be a very good instrument for the movement of inequality in many different situations.

Why does this work? A moment's thought can help make it clear. Suppose we take a large country like China. It is well known that inequality in China rose during the period of economic reforms, as the cities grew rich much more rapidly than the countryside. This will show up clearly in an inter-provincial measure of inequality in China! Similarly, certain economic sectors (finance, transport, utilities) had income gains far exceeding those of farmers or factory workers. This too will show up in an inter-sectoral measure. Taking the two together, and using sectors-within-provinces as the category structure, one can obtain a very detailed picture of the trends that dominate the movement of Chinese inequalities over time (Figure 5.3).

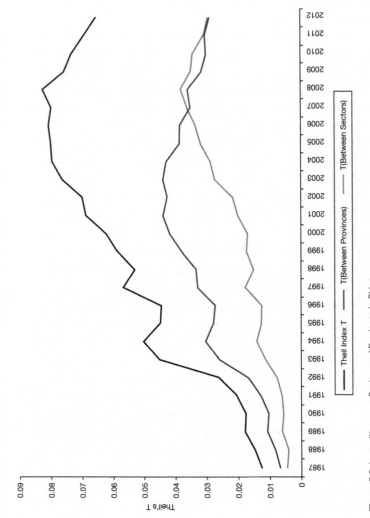

Figure 5.3 Inequality across Sectors and Provinces in China
Calculation by Wenjie Zhang. Used with permission.

Yes, it may be true that inequalities within a sector-within-a-province—among schoolteachers in Hebei, for instance—were also growing. But that is clearly going to be a small matter compared to the differences between bank executives in Shanghai and herdsmen in Tibet.

So long as one has a consistent grouping scheme that stays relatively constant over time, the between-groups Theil T method can be used to generate useful time series of inequality for many countries. In this respect, geographical data work well, since borders tend to change only rarely and since all competent governments are interested in collecting tariffs and taxes and in knowing what is going on in their economies. What is less clear is why the same trick should work for sectoral data measured using the same category scheme in different countries—with data taken (for instance) from the Industrial Statistics of the United Nations Industrial Development Organization or from Eurostat's REGIO data base. But it appears that the standardization of categories does have the effect of making the between-groups component of Theil's T comparable across countries, since the upper bound of the between-groups component is determined by the number of groups. And this is a great advantage, even over computing the underlying Theil from population data, since the underlying Theil (unlike the Gini) is not bounded by 100 or any other value, but will generally rise with an increasing population size.

For about twenty years, this author has been running a research project that involves computing Theil's T statistics and turning them into global inequality data sets. We still haven't run out of fresh ideas.

6

CAUSES OF CHANGING INEQUALITY IN THE UNITED STATES

A half-century ago, the study of economic inequality was moribund in the United States. Indeed, in 1958 John Kenneth Galbraith noted in *The Affluent Society* that "few things are more evident in modern social history than the decline of interest in inequality as an economic issue." Thanks to the New Deal and the progressive income tax, American society had become egalitarian, at least by previous standards, and so it seemed likely to remain. In the 1970s, when this author reached graduate school, the study of inequality was still characterized by his teachers as like "watching the grass grow."

Today, few things are more evident in modern social history than the revival of interest in inequality. The revival began in the late 1980s, propelled by a book called *The Great U-Turn* by economists Barry Bluestone and Bennett Harrison. It blossomed in the 1990s into a debate over the sources of rising inequality, and settled in the 2000s into trench warfare between the proponents of opposing views. Today that debate has subsided, without having actually been resolved. The contestants have moved on to argue over the meaning and

For a comprehensive guide to the 1990s debates, see Galbraith, James K., *Created Unequal.*

consequences of rising inequality, which we shall take up in a later chapter.

From a scientific standpoint, it is strange to isolate a single country—even the United States—as the focal point for the discussion of any economic topic. Inequality is a worldwide phenomenon, and if economics is a science, the causes of changing inequality should not be that different from one country to the next. However, American economics is inward-looking and self-absorbed—and the United States does have some special characteristics. We have little choice but to take the debate on inequality in the United States as a somewhat distinct topic from the analysis of inequalities in the wider world. So for the sake of convenience, if nothing else, we treat them in separate chapters.

The debate over rising inequality in the United States took shape with the publication in 1993 of an article by John Bound and George Johnson in the *American Economic Review*, and a book in 1994 by the British economist Adrian Wood. The hypotheses offered in those works were based on conventional economic and trade theory, and were made with limited empirical evidence. At the time, the evidence was largely restricted to survey-type micro-studies, conducted at two or more widely separated dates, that showed an increase over time in the relative earnings of those who had more years of education. This led to an early concentration on the question of technology and "returns to skill."

How Does Technology Affect Inequality?

In a classical supply-and-demand model of the labor market, employers hire workers up to the point where the cost of adding a new worker—which is the wage—just offsets the benefit to the employer of making the hire. Now suppose there are two types of workers, "skilled" and "unskilled." A simple variation on this theory holds that each type will be hired up to the point where the benefit (or marginal product) just offsets the wage, and since the marginal products will differ, so will the wages.

Now suppose that some technological change—never mind, for the moment, exactly what—occurs, which raises the marginal productivity of the more skilled group of workers. In that case, the theory predicts a rise in the equilibrium wage for skilled workers, and no change in the equilibrium wage for unskilled workers. Inequality increases. This is called "skill-biased technological change."

Bound and Johnson's simple idea was that some technical change of this type had occurred. Most economists, then and later, assumed or inferred that the change in question must have been the rise of computerization. No direct showing of this was made, however, and some later papers contradicted it. One careful study, for instance, found that while using computers was indeed associated with a higher wage, so was using a pencil, or sitting in a chair. That would leave open the possibility that easy-to-observe *status*, rather than hard-to-measure productivity, is the major factor affecting pay and also access to toys and perks inside large organizations.

When one considers simple evidence, it should be clear why the notion that the *use* of new technologies drives wages led to a dead end. First, consider how computers and other new technologies are actually used. They are (first of all) mass products, mainly (these days) for personal consumption. But on the production side, they are used to replace *unskilled* labor, and also to permit the substitution of unskilled for skilled labor, for example at telephone switchboards and checkout counters. In neither case does the use of the machines require or reward skills. If they increase inequality, it's by depressing all wages *except* for those of certain skilled workers whose jobs cannot (yet) be computerized. Those jobs may not require big brains; they may instead rely on nimble fingers or (as with jobs in the caring professions) a simple human touch.

But even for those who found the skill-bias hypothesis attractive, there were still alternatives to explore and other possibilities to refute. In particular, it had to be shown that the demand for skill had risen in relationship to the supply of skill. And it had to be shown that the increasing gap between skilled and unskilled groups could not be attributed to some other cause, such as an increasing relative supply of *less skilled* workers.

Of course, to supply skill is the task of education.

How Does Education Affect Inequality?

The economics of markets is a game of supply and demand; having more of any commodity on offer means that it will trade at a lower price. If skills are a commodity supplied by education, then it is a good thing for the skilled if they are scarce and a bad thing if they are common. By this reasoning, investment in education is wise for the individual, since it raises individual skills and therefore access to better jobs. But if pursued by too many people, that investment will lose its value, as the market becomes glutted with qualified applicants for the best and most technically sophisticated jobs.

The argument that skill-bias in technical change produced rising inequality is thus an argument that the pace of new technology exceeded the ability of the schools to supply the necessary skills. A difficulty is that there are no independent measures of either "the pace of technology" or of the "new supply of skills." So the argument proceeds by inference, from the mere fact that the wage premium paid to people with more years of schooling seems to have risen. If inequality is rising— and if the model is correct—that must mean that technology is "winning the race" with education. If inequality should fall, that would mean that education must be catching up.

How does the skill-biased technological change argument hold up over time? The answer is, very poorly. It originated in the 1980s when in the United States inequality rose especially in the early part of the decade. But that was before the large-scale introduction of micro-computers, supposedly the driving force! In the late 1990s, when the new technologies exploded, it was later discovered that while income inequality did rise, *pay* inequalities fell—and the theory applies to pay, not to income. In the first two decades of the twenty-first century, while some economists still cling to the "SBTC" argument, they do so mainly because they have learned to defer to mainstream theory, not because any new evidence has come to the rescue.

Finally, the idea that increasing the supply of certain skill categories reduces their wage advantage—while seemingly logical—does not reflect how wage structures in an advanced economy really work. If it were true, then the vast number of college students who took degrees in computer science during and after the information-technology boom should have depressed the pay flowing to those who work in the leading-edge companies of the high-technology sector. There is no evidence that this is the case.

Compared to the number of computer science graduates, the numbers who get work in the high end of the sector is very, very small, and their pay remains, on the whole, very high. Why is this so? Because those companies compete with each other in a winner-take-all system for shares of sales and profits in constantly evolving market space. To do that, they have to pay top dollar for the best talent, and they have no interest in nickel-and-diming their technical workforce if that might mean a loss of morale or the departure of top staff. Instead, there is a ferocious competition for the jobs, and those who do not get them must take secondary employment or find something else to do with their lives—driving taxis, for instance (or for Uber), a functional outlet for educated people of all types who cannot find a job in their original line of work.[1]

1. I am, however, reliably told that very few PhDs actually drive taxis in America. Still, a recent study of three developing countries finds a similar effect: as college education grows, those with only secondary education are forced down the occupation and pay scale. See Mehta et al. in the Bibliography.

What Are the Effects of Trade on Inequality?

For a time in the 1990s, the chief competitor to the skill-bias hypothesis was the idea that trade—specifically, North-South trade, or trade between rich and poorer countries—was the driving force behind increasing inequality in the structure of wages and income.

While technology is supposed to work on the demand side of the labor market equation, trade is supposed to work on the supply side. By opening up one's borders to trade in manufactured goods with developing countries—the argument goes—one is obliged to compete with firms in countries that may have few skilled workers but that can pay much lower wages to unskilled workers. This expands the effective supply of unskilled workers in the home market, places competitive pressure on home-country firms, and works to drive down their wages.

Beyond question, manufacturing workers in the United States, especially those in the heavily unionized states of the North and Midwest, faced major competitive pressures from the 1970s onward. These came first from Germany and Japan, then from Korea, then Mexico, and a bit later from China and other places as trade expanded and became more global, and as free-trade agreements such as the NAFTA were introduced. They also came, to a degree, from non-unionized competition in the American South, from new investment by domestic and foreign companies in states such as Tennessee, Alabama, and South Carolina.

But manufacturing jobs constitute only a small part of US employment (then perhaps 15 percent, now about 8), and within that sector wage concessions were not the main response to competitive pressures. Instead, factories moved, workers lost their jobs, taking less-well-paid ones elsewhere if they could get them, and eventually retiring from the workforce. The lower wages that would show up in a survey were therefore a consequence of a changing

composition of jobs rather than of wage adjustments in particular jobs—a distinction easily lost on survey-takers and
economists but quite evident to the people experiencing
the transition. Meanwhile the services sector expanded,
and the demographic structure of the workforce changed,
with more women, more minorities, more young workers,
and more immigrants. These workers were less skilled and
less well paid than those they replaced—but on the other
hand, they were better off personally than before they
found work.

Adrian Wood's 1994 book made a careful calculation of the
statistical effect of trade on the overall wage structure, and
concluded that the direct effect of lost jobs in manufacturing
could account for only a fraction of the increasing gap between
skilled and unskilled workers. He then estimated that two
other factors might have amplified that effect: defensive labor-
saving by US producers faced with foreign competition, and
unmeasured competition in the services sector. Plausible
estimates of these factors would expand the effect of trade to
account for nearly all of increasing wage inequality, at least
up to that time. However, these effects were speculative, and
most economists remained skeptical. Wood's argument also
required that rising inequality in the United States be counter-
balanced by falling inequalities in developing-country trading
partners—and later analysis of international data showed that
this quite definitely was not the case.

All in all, the expansion of global trading networks and
so-called "free trade agreements" in the 1990s and early 2000s
engendered passionate opposition, in part due to arguments
about the effect of North-South trade on wages. Yet in retro-
spect the effect of expanding trade on wages in the United
States is limited by the small scale of the manufacturing sector, and by the limited capacity of older firms and factories
to defend themselves against outside competition simply by
cutting wages.

Another argument held that the lifting of the Iron Curtain, caused by the collapse of the Soviet Union in 1992, opened up a world of cheap but highly skilled labor to Western and especially to American companies. There is no doubt that for a time Soviet scientists, mathematicians, and technologists could be had on the global market for a fraction of what it would have cost to hire comparable talent grown at home. But if this were a significant force on inequalities of pay within the West, the effect would be to lower them, by reducing wages at the very high end of the structure. There is no evidence of such an effect. On the contrary, in the financial sector to which many of the best mathematicians migrated, the fall of the Soviet Union coincided with the start of a golden age of quantitative finance and increasing incomes in the sector—all as a prelude to eventual disaster.

As for manufacturing, the larger reality seems to be that newer technologies in new locations win out in the end, and that lower wages are only a small part of that competitive struggle, in which the rising powers of Asia have taken such a strong position over the past generation. To the extent that trade increased pay inequality in the United States, it did so mainly by substituting new foreign production facilities for those that previously existed in-country, and therefore transforming the structure of the US economy, taking away a previously powerful middle section and leaving behind a small high-end (some of that supplied by immigrant talent) and a large low-end (some of that also supplied by immigrants). This is not the mechanism of "wage adjustment" specified in the standard models.

What Are the Effects of Migration on Inequality?

Immigrants often get blamed for declining unskilled wages; the argument is again a simple supply-and-demand one, in which an increasing supply of non-natives willing to work for low wages drives down the equilibrium wage in those segments of the labor market for which immigrants can supply qualified labor. These include farm labor, construction, hotel and restaurant services, janitorial and housework, and low-end factory jobs, especially in the food-processing sector. In past times, the power of this argument was sufficient to motivate trade unions to take a strongly anti-immigrant position, in the interest of protecting their own wages.

Here again, however, there is a plausible counterargument, which rests on the fact that unorganized workers have very little leverage over their wages, and also takes note of the fact that the United States does have a federal minimum wage, with state and city minima that are in many cases somewhat higher. (For instance, while the federal minimum has been stuck at $7.25 per hour, California in 2014 enacted a statewide minimum of $10 per hour, and Los Angeles city has voted to go to $15 per hour gradually.)

The alternative idea is that low wages, and in particular a low minimum wage, have the effect of making it profitable for employers to seek out migrant workers. The reason is simple: when the minimum is very low, it is very hard to find competent native workers to take the jobs, outside perhaps certain carefully supervised work environments suitable for teenagers and (increasingly) young adults, such as coffee houses and fast food restaurants. Therefore, employers seek out migrant and immigrant employees—often without legal documentation—who will take the work and cause very little trouble, since they are liable always to worry about the possibility of detention and deportation. Conversely, a much higher minimum wage would make bad jobs attractive to citizens, and therefore reduce (especially illegal) immigration.

Does immigration cause low wages, or do low wages cause immigration? It is not easy to distinguish the two models with coarse evidence, but there are some ways. Some years ago, in an exchange with Professor Christopher Jencks on the letters page of *The New York Review of Books*, this author noted that Cambridge, Massachusetts, has two major universities, Harvard and MIT, separated by about twenty minutes' walk. If the labor market functioned as mainstream economic theory suggests, they should not have different starting wages for janitorial staff. Yet they did: even though Harvard is a much richer institution, MIT's starting wage for janitors was about six dollars per hour higher. A prediction of the alternative theory would be that Harvard would hire a more vulnerable, easier-to-manage, more-immigrant labor force than would MIT, even though MIT clearly could have had access to the same cheap labor as Harvard, had it wanted to take advantage. I was not able to verify this prediction except through the casual observation of colleagues at both institutions.

How Does Government Affect Inequality?

Major forces behind wage structures and the inequality of disposable incomes are the political and social institutions that create and maintain those structures in the first place. These include above all the government, the trade unions, and private for-profit corporations.

The government affects the structure of wage inequality in two major ways. First, it maintains a minimum wage, which in the United States has little practical effect because it is so low that only a handful of workers are affected by it. However, in other countries where the minimum is higher, and in past times in the United States, the minimum wage places a significant floor under pay to normally low-paid groups, especially minorities and women, and in regions of the country where costs are low. It thus is a force against both categorical and regional inequalities.

The second way the government affects pay structures is by maintaining standards for work funded from public sources. Part of this is simply the pay scale for government employees, which tends to place upward pressure on wage rates for similar jobs in the private sector. And provisions of federal law require that construction contracts funded by the government pay the "prevailing wage" in the area, which is usually taken to mean union rates. In these ways, the government has an important influence over substantial parts of the private-sector wage structure.

Government also determines the gap that may exist between inequalities of gross income and those of net or disposable income. It does this in two ways: by specifying progressive tax structures that curb the incomes of the relatively wealthy, and by creating transfer and social insurance programs that support the incomes of those who are not well provided for with private funds. In all of the advanced countries, including the United States, the inequalities of gross incomes are reduced substantially by these programs.

Since around 1980, there have been substantial changes in tax law in the United States. How have these affected inequality? The answer may be surprising. Inequality of gross incomes in the United States seems to have risen about six Gini points from 1980 until around 1994, according to a variety of studies. But inequalities of net income grew a bit less than that, perhaps around four to five Gini points. So it seems that on balance the tax system worked, during this period, to moderate the rise in gross income inequalities that was due to other factors during those years. After 1994, the inequality of income from work in the United States, both gross and net, seems to have been fairly stable; rising inequalities in tax records appear to stem heavily from capital income.

Of course, this was a period of major changes in the tax code, favoring the rich for the most part. So what happened? First, it appears that the cuts in tax rates on top incomes had the effect of offsetting income-tax "bracket creep," which would have made the system even more progressive had nothing been done. Part of those pro-rich tax cuts merely maintained the redistributive status quo, while pre-tax inequality was rising. Second, there were some changes, most notably an expanded Earned Income Tax Credit, that markedly improved the incomes of the very lowest-paid workers, and that took some of the burden previously borne by the welfare system, and delivered it through the tax system instead. This would help to account for a slightly slower increase of post-tax, compared to pre-tax, inequalities, and perhaps even for a decline in post-tax, post-transfer inequalities noted for the United States in some of the most recent studies.

How Do Trade Unions Affect Inequality?

Trade union membership grew rapidly in the 1930s and 1940s, with the passage of the National Labor Relations Act and the Fair Labor Standards Act, and with the industrial mobilization that accompanied the Second World War. By the end of that war, the United States was by far the largest industrial power in the world, and trade union membership was around 30 percent of the employed labor force. At that time, major collective bargaining arrangements in automobiles, steel, rubber, and chemicals helped to set the standard for wage increases throughout the economy, and by the 1960s it was national policy that workers should receive, each year, a wage increase equal to the rate of productivity growth. The power of unions and their role in national wage-setting policy helped to assure an ongoing stability, or even decline, in the inequality of the wage and pay structures through the 1960s.

But American dominance of world manufacturing was inevitably a short-term phenomenon, destined to erode as Europe and Japan recovered from the war, and then to erode further as industrial development took hold elsewhere. American strategic policy fostered that recovery, particularly as Germany and Japan were front-line states in the Cold War, so that giving Japan, in particular, access to American consumer markets was a part of the international security framework. Later, the same logic would apply to South Korea, and ironically, the arrangements created for those countries would eventually extend to the People's Republic of China and the Democratic Republic of Vietnam.

Quite apart from trade and strategic considerations, union strength never extended into the American South, and productivity growth in any event progressively reduced the labor requirements of the manufacturing sector, so that new employment became increasingly centered on decentralized services and construction. There were, in addition, scandals of governance in certain unions, notably the mine workers just before the center of coal mining moved from West Virginia and Eastern Kentucky to Wyoming, and in trucking just before Congress deregulated the trucking sector in 1979. Union coverage and power declined, and in the early 1980s it received a massive blow from the industrial recession of that period, combined with the powerful attack on worker rights and standing that was launched by the administration of Ronald Reagan. By the time of the Great Recession of 2008, manufacturing employment had fallen to about 8 percent of the workforce, and union coverage to only 6 percent of the working population. The effect of private sector unions on wages was still important in a handful of industries, but the countervailing power of the union movement in national terms, and its ability to influence the overall distribution of pay in the United States, had been gravely diminished.

A notable exception to the decline of unions in the United States over the past generation has been the rapid growth of unions in the public sector. Public sector unions trace their roots back to the union organization of postal clerks in the 1890s, but strong growth only began in the 1960s, with the support of the Kennedy administration. By 2009 there were more union members in the public than in the private sector, and public sector unions, especially teachers' unions, were coming under severe attack. This has been especially the case in industrial states, such as Wisconsin and Indiana, where industrial decline has weakened the industrial unions and has strengthened the relative position of conservative political forces, but also in states like New York and cities like Chicago, where political leaders in the Democratic Party and the public sector unions are estranged. In California, on the other hand, the public sector unions remain strong.

Under the Clinton and Obama administrations, trade unions have attempted to reduce the barriers to forming unions, to extend the reach of unions in the services sector, to raise the minimum wage, and to support the struggles of immigrant workers. At present writing, union efforts to raise the minimum wage to $15 per hour appear to have gathered strength around the country, with major cities including Seattle and Los Angeles enacting such legislation. However, the political climate remains extremely difficult for workers' organizations.

How Have Family-Structure Changes Affected Inequality?

In the wake of the Second World War, national policy encouraged women to abandon the labor force, move to the suburbs with their ex-GI partners, and form families. Meanwhile, Social Security (and later Medicare and Medicaid) made it possible for the older generation to remain independent. The iconic American middle-class family, as a mass phenomenon, probably dates only from this period—a nuclear family for the atomic age. Especially in rural America, before that time, extended families were the norm, as several generations were obliged to share the same space and to depend on each other.

But the nuclear family, it turns out, is not an eternal or stable form. And in the 1970s and 1980s it received a hard blow from the industrial recessions of those years, which cut away the incomes of a substantial part of the better-paid working class, almost all of which consisted of male heads of household. (This was especially true for African American workingmen in the Midwest, where the automotive industry had only recently given a substantial part of that population a foothold in middle-class stability.) The result was a significant reorganization of family structures that continued through the 1980s, even though the economy as a whole recovered from the recessions of the previous decade.

The effect of that reorganization was to create a larger number of families headed by a single, low-income female parent, heavily dependent on informal wages, food assistance, and welfare benefits. It also encouraged "assortative mating"—giving a strong income advantage to households with two or more working partners who could pool their incomes. The former group sank to the bottom of the overall income distribution, while the latter group rose toward the top, and both phenomena increased overall household income inequality. So even though pay inequalities stabilized after 1983, the ripple effect of the disruption continued to increase household income inequalities for the rest of the decade at least. And then, in the late 1980s, another recession compounded the stresses on working households.

How Do Corporate Structures, the Stock Market, and Capital Asset Bubbles Affect Inequality?

One further source of institutional change has had a profound effect on gross income inequality in the United States—and is distinctive, largely, to the United States. That is the change in corporate structures and the dominant modes of corporate finance since the early 1980s, and the rise of the stock market and other capital asset prices.

In the early postwar period, the dominant American industrial corporation—such as General Motors, General Electric, American Telephone & Telegraph, International Business Machines—was an integrated behemoth that contained within itself not only production, but every phase of basic research, product design, and marketing that was relevant to its mission. Therefore incomes were distributed within the corporation by administrative decisions, governed by the bureaucratic imperatives and prerogatives of those in charge, and strongly responsive to the incentives of a highly progressive income tax structure. Top scientists and engineers, as well as top executives, were paid salaries, and salaries were regulated by the corporation. Tax structures also gave strong incentives for the corporation to retain profits, rather than pay them out as dividends, and to reinvest the proceeds—whether in factories or in the palatial towers that grew up in Manhattan, San Francisco, and Chicago in those years.

All of this changed with the tax "reform" movements of the 1970s and 1980s, which pushed for lower top marginal tax rates, fewer special exemptions from the tax, and for a "shareholder-value" model of corporate compensation. And a special feature of this change was that it created strong incentives to restructure the corporation itself.

In particular, as the digital revolution came into view, the top technologists in the big corporations realized that they would be far better off if they set off on their own, incorporated themselves as independent technology firms, and then sold their output back to the companies for which they had formerly worked in salaried jobs. In that way, technologists could become owners, taking advantage of venture finance, and could, in effect, upset the previous structure of American corporate valuation. Fairchild Semiconductor is the firm commonly credited with pioneering this model, and the "Fairchildren" soon followed, of which the most prominent is the now-dominant micro-processor manufacturing firm, Intel. Microsoft, Apple, Oracle, and now Google, along with many others, have followed a similar path, though of course the details differ and the trajectories continue to evolve.

The effect of this structural transformation on the distribution of household incomes in the United States, as recorded in the tax records, is astonishing. For there were created, mainly in the 1990s, a handful of citadels of stratospheric incomes, previously unknown in the country and concentrated in a tiny handful of locations. One of these was Manhattan, the home of Wall Street and the source of finance. A second was Silicon Valley, a cluster of counties in Northern California. And the third was Seattle, Washington, and its near suburbs. After that, the income gains extend to another ten or so counties scattered around the country, before falling off dramatically everywhere else.

If one removes just five counties from a Theil measure of the inequality of incomes between counties for the years 1993 to 2000, it turns out that the growth of personal income inequality in tax records, measured across counties—which reached a peak in 2000 with the NASDAQ boom—falls by half. The five counties are New York (New York), Santa Clara, San Mateo, and San Francisco (California), and King County (Washington). Remove fifteen counties and the growth of personal income inequality in the 1990s, as captured in this measure, just about disappears.

Figure 6.1 shows the average income of the top 1 percent in the United States alongside the average income of the bottom 90 percent. It is very clear that the peaks, valleys, and again peaks at the top coincide with the movement of the stock market and real estate boom and bust. Personal income inequality in the United States peaked in 2000, and then declined with the information-technology bust that followed. It rose again, to a new peak just about as high, in the mortgage-finance scandal that preceded the Great Financial Crisis in 2008. But the geographic locations (and therefore presumably the beneficiaries) of the boom income were different—apart from the Wall Street financiers, who remained at the top of the pile. In this second great bubble, incomes grew rapidly in a number of scattered locations, including Florida and Southern California, where there was a great deal of shadily financed residential construction. Then this too went away. A third peak seems to

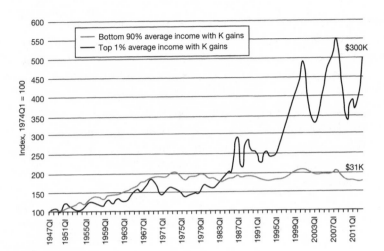

Figure 6.1 Top 1 Percent and Bottom 90 Percent Average Incomes, United States, 1947–2012

Credit: Olivier Giovannoni. Used with permission.

have occurred, perhaps in 2013, with the stock market recovery following the Great Crisis.

No doubt a geographic analysis will show the newest income titans to be located heavily in the shale patch, as the prosperity of Texas, nighttime gas flares in North Dakota, and a shiny new office building in Oklahoma City can attest. What will happen if oil prices now stay low is another matter.

The United States is a large, rich, and complex country, with an ever-evolving economic structure. It is perhaps not surprising that to understand well the course of events—and the evolution of a measure of income inequalities in such a country—it is necessary to study political and economic events in fine detail. It is therefore also not surprising that simple stories cooked up out of the imagination of economists do not hold up very well. It is a great advantage that in studying the United States, a rich body of data exists that can help us arrive somewhat more closely at a reasonable account.

In the case of the world economy, complexities mount even further, and the quality of the data available declines. As we take up this larger topic in the following chapter, we will find ourselves pressed to seek out plausible, simple explanations for the intricate patterns we observe. Fortunately, access to comparative information for multiple countries provides a way to approach this problem, which is not available when one is studying any one country alone.

7

CAUSES OF CHANGING INEQUALITY IN THE WORLD

When we move toward an analysis of inequalities in the wider world, we are required to cope with far more complex and uncertain data, and at the same time to seek simpler and more abstract theories. With some 220 extant countries, if each one spawned its own narratives, as the rise of inequality in the United States has done, we would never get anywhere. But to come up with a theory that has common application across many countries, we need measurements of inequality across countries and through time that are reasonably comprehensive and reasonably reliable—and this is a major challenge.

What Do We Know about Inequality in the Whole World?

Leaving aside efforts to construct a single measure of inequality for the world's population (see Chapter 4), there are a number of major data sets that have collected Gini coefficients for a wide range of countries and years, almost entirely restricted to the period since 1950, and for the most part to much more recent years.

The great early effort along these lines was by Klaus Deininger and Lyn Squire at the World Bank, who in 1995 released a compendium of over 700 "high-quality" Gini coefficients, along with many others that they deemed less reliable.

The coefficients came from many sources, some public sector but many based on surveys conducted by nongovernmental research organizations. Coverage was sparse and weighted to the rich countries; even 700 coefficients spread unevenly over 220 countries will leave many with little or no reported information. Concepts differed; the measures were sometimes gross and sometimes net of tax, sometimes based on household units and sometimes on persons, sometimes based on income and sometimes on expenditure. As a result, it was very difficult for researchers using the *Deininger-Squire* (DS) data set to arrive at consistent and credible conclusions as to what the data actually showed.

The DS data set has since been incorporated into the work of the World Institute for Development Economics Research (WIDER) of the United Nations University in Helsinki, which has added greatly to the database. Problems of coverage have been reduced, but the difficulties of differing concepts and uncertain comparability across measures remain. The DS and WIDER efforts are perhaps best viewed as vital repositories of past studies, rather than as polished comparative data sets. They are compendia of work done by hundreds of different research teams around the world over the years; it is not a criticism to state that when the underlying measures and calculations differ, the resulting data have to be treated with caution.

The World Bank has since moved on, and now publishes a "Gini coefficient" as part of the *World Development Indicators* (WDI) reported annually by the Bank. The actual genesis of and concepts underlying these coefficients are not as clearly distinguished as they might be—for instance, expenditure and income measures, which are definitely not comparable, are presented side by side. And the coverage is very sparse, so that the WDI cannot be considered a serious comparative research data set.

The *Luxembourg Income Study* (LIS) take a different approach, one of meticulous comparison of micro data sets accumulated from the original sources and available for micro studies of all kinds. Summary measures of household income inequality (market, gross, and net) from the LIS are considered to be among the most trustworthy available for comparative research. But coverage (though growing) is still small by world standards, with an emphasis on a handful of recent years in the wealthier countries.

Thomas Piketty of the Paris School of Economics and his associates Emmanuel Saez, Anthony Atkinson, and Gabriel Zucman attempt to build measures of *top income shares* from tax data in a selection of countries. These measures are not measures of inequality, since they reflect just a single point (the share in total taxable income of the top 10 percent or 1 percent, or 0.1 or 0.01 percent) of the distribution. But they are a useful complement to inequality measures, since the movement of the top shares reflects, to a degree, the overall movement of income inequality.

The advantage of the top share data sets is a long run of data for a few of the world's wealthiest countries, including the United States, the United Kingdom, France, and Germany. Disadvantages include the fact that there are only twenty-nine countries in the data set, that it is restricted to countries with income tax records, and that comparability across countries is limited by differences in the definition of income and in the effectiveness of tax enforcement. Comparability across time is also something to be treated cautiously, since countries constantly rewrite their legal definitions of taxable income.

Moving in a different direction, Frederick Solt of the University of Iowa has produced a very large *Standardized World Income Inequality Data* set (SWIID), giving about 7,000 estimates each of market and net income inequality for 174 countries in a recent update. The SWIID has achieved wide acceptance; it was used, for instance, in recent studies by the International Monetary Fund. But some scholars remain skeptical, since the SWIID draws on many distinct sources and is not based in all cases on actual measurement. Rather, many reported observations are generated by imputation—by filling in missing values based on observations in neighboring places and neighboring times. This makes statistical work with the SWIID problematic, since there are fewer independent observations than the data set reports. The SWIID appears broadly consistent with the actual surveys on which it is based, but does exhibit some strange behavior, in countries and for years where actual observations are sparse, often in the early or late years of a series.

My own effort along these lines is the *Estimated Household Income Inequality* (EHII) data set of the University of Texas Inequality Project. EHII is a collection of Gini coefficients for gross household income inequality. It is based on actual measurements of *pay* inequality in the industrial sector, using the between-groups component of Theil's T statistic computed from the United Nations Industrial Development Organization (UNIDO) compilation of payroll and employment by industry for countries around the world. These are then converted into Gini format using the close statistical relationship between the measured T statistic and the original Deininger-Squire Gini measures, for about 430 overlapping observations. The result is a single-concept, consistent comparative data set with (at latest revision) 3,872 estimates for 149 countries. The EHII estimates track actual measures of gross household income inequality in many countries quite well, and with many more observations than can be garnered directly from surveys. We will use this data for comparative purposes in the following sections.

How Is Inequality Related to Economic Development?

Theories of economic development took off in the years following the Second World War, in part to meet the ideological challenges facing capitalism in the post-colonial countries during the Cold War. For those countries, communism offered a dual promise: rapid industrialization, as pioneered by the Soviet

Union, and an egalitarian society run by representatives of the working classes and not by foreign firms or local puppets of the old masters. The communists also rejected social stratification on the basis of race or sex, liberating people of color and women from long histories of oppression. It was not obvious, to many observers, that capitalist society could prove itself an attractive alternative in a world where it was no longer considered good manners to impose the choice of economic system by brute force.

In this climate the economist Simon Kuznets offered an idea based on a simple model of industrial and structural change. Suppose one starts (as in the Northern states of the United States before the Civil War) with an agrarian society based on family farms and small freeholds. Then industrialization begins. Industry engenders and depends on cities, which grow up around the new factories and mills. Wages in factories must exceed the living one can earn on the farm, or workers will not accept that employment. So the cities are wealthier than the countryside. Inequality, originally very low, must increase as urbanization and industrialization proceed.

But, Kuznets then argued, there eventually will come a turning point. At some point, as agriculture becomes mechanized, the population of the countryside will diminish to a small fraction of the total. Then the inequalities that matter will no longer be those that distinguish the city from the hinterland, but those that exist within the cities. These, while initially high, will diminish as the working classes organize, vote, and create for themselves a world of unionized collective bargaining and, in the political sphere, social democracy and the welfare state. As income rises, inequality will decline, and the ultimate destiny of industrial capitalism is a society of tolerably egalitarian qualities, without the violence necessarily associated with communist revolution.

Kuznets's idea was based on a core insight: the major forces affecting inequality in the process of economic development are not specific public policies, but the structural relations of different sectors in the economy as development unfolds. Certain aspects of the evolution of inequalities are inevitable. Two forces come into play: the relative weight in population and activity of high- and low-income sectors, and the differential in relative pay between them. If the historical process unfolds as Kuznets described, then the trajectory of inequality will follow an inverted U-curve, first rising and then falling as average income grows.

This insight may be modified if the initial or the terminal conditions are different from those that Kuznets assumed. For instance, suppose that instead of egalitarian homesteaders, the initial agriculture is one of large plantations worked by slave labor? In that case, industrialization might decrease inequality, even if the plantations persist, since the industrial element would comprise a previously nonexistent middle class. In that case, the "Kuznets curve" might be entirely downward sloping, with an egalitarian society emerging steadily in the course of growth, development, and emergent resistance to the most repellent features of the previous structure.

Or again, suppose that there emerges a trend toward globalization, under which some countries take the lead in providing advanced technologies, capital equipment, and services such as communications, insurance, and finance? In that case, inequality may rise in those advanced countries with further growth in income, which will flow in the first instance to the few, well-paid denizens of the advanced sectors. The Kuznets curve, having declined during an initial, national phase of industrialization, will now rise in the richest countries as the new international phase takes shape. In a paper in 2000, Pedro Conçeicão and this author christened this possibility the "Augmented Kuznets Curve" (Figure 7.1). It appears to fit the evidence quite well for the United States, the United Kingdom, and Japan.

How does the broader evidence fit the Kuznets curve? Many economists, using DS or WIDER, have concluded that

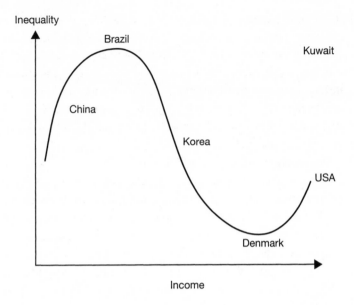

Figure 7.1 The Augmented Kuznets Curve

the fit is poor. The University of Texas Inequality Project (UTIP) team, using measures of *pay* inequality from the UTIP-UNIDO data set, takes a more favorable view. Kuznets himself stressed that his theory was one related to pay, rather than to income, and so it is reasonable to focus on this type of data. The UTIP-UNIDO data suggest that most countries are on a declining Kuznets surface, but that China is on an upward-sloping surface for the traditional reasons, while a few advanced countries, including the United States, are again on an upward-sloping surface for the novel reasons just given. Underrating Simon Kuznets is not a good idea.

How Do Political Systems, Violence, Revolution, and War Affect Inequality?

If there are world forces that affect the rise or decline of economic inequality, does that mean that local conditions and institutions are unimportant? Of course not. For an appropriate analogy, consider a coastal area ravaged by a massive storm. The extent of the damage will depend in part on the strength of the storm. But it will also depend on the lay of the land, and on the strength of the levees, dikes, and ocean gates that may be in place when the storm hits. Similarly, as the world economy is swept by violent forces, the effect on individual countries will depend in part on their institutions and on their policies—on whether they accept or resist.

With a good comparative data set, such as EHII or UTIP-UNIDO, it becomes possible to assess the effect of particular political systems and of distinct events, such as war and revolutions, on the course of inequality. However, to make useful conclusions about these matters, one also needs a good source of information about political systems, wars, and revolutions. These data sets are largely the province of political scientists, who developed them for other purposes. In the case of the major data sets covering political systems (the POLITY data sets) there is a problem, which is that the scale runs from "authoritarian" to "democratic," grouping communist and fascist regimes, or military dictatorships, in the same category. But it is clear that with respect to inequality, these two types of authoritarianism are quite different.

Hsu (2008) addressed this problem by developing a categorical data set of regime types by country and year, using a wide range of descriptors to capture the ideology and institutional characteristics of different countries at different times. This permits the data to indicate whether there are significant differences between countries at different times, according to their political regimes.

It turns out, not surprisingly, that there are significant differences between levels of inequality observed in countries with different political systems. Communist countries (in their day) had low inequality, as Cuba does to the present day. The social democratic governments of northern Europe retained low inequalities at least into the first decade of the 2000s, although values may have changed in recent years in certain cases. Islamic republics have somewhat lower degrees of inequality than their income levels would otherwise suggest. On the other hand, military regimes and one-party non-communist dictatorships tend to have inequality measures on the high side. When military regimes and dictatorships come to an end, inequality is generally much higher than it was before, and the restoration of democracy does not immediately, or automatically, bring a reduction. It takes a long time (if ever) for a newly established democratic government to begin to reduce inequalities incurred under a previous regime, as elected governments in South Africa, Brazil, Chile, and elsewhere have discovered.

It is also possible to assess the effect on inequality of historical events within particular countries. There was, for instance, a spectacular rise in inequality in the countries of Eastern Europe and the former Soviet Union when the Cold War ended and the Soviet Union broke up. Revolutions are rare events in modern data, but we note a sharp decline in inequality in Iran following the revolution there. There also appears to have been, as a general rule, declining inequality in periods just before right-wing coups d'état, and rising inequality thereafter; this was the experience of Chile before and after 1973, of Argentina before and after 1976, and of numerous other experiences that may be tracked in the data.

How Do Interest Rates, Growth, and Saving Affect Inequality?

Most theories of increasing inequality explored so far have been *microeconomic*; their core idea is that outside forces, such as technology or trade, buffet incomes through the mediation of particular markets for labor time and capital assets. Kuznets's theory is *meso-economic*, meaning that it relates to structural change across grand categories of economic activity and development.

In 2014 Thomas Piketty offered a simple *macroeconomic* theory of rising inequality, based on two "fundamental laws." The first was based on the fact that the ownership of financial assets is concentrated, and so if income on financial assets rises faster than income in general, then the inequality of income should increase. If we call income on financial assets (which is their interest rate) r, and the growth rate of income g, Piketty argued that typical value for r is around 5 percent per year, while that for g is closer to 2 percent, over the long run. Thus, $r > g$. We will return to this later.

A high interest rate surely favors creditors, and a low one favors debtors. It is equally sure that "people who have money to lend tend to have more money, than people who do not have money to lend."[1] So we should expect periods of high interest rates to favor the rich and periods of low interest rates to favor the poor. We shall discuss some global evidence for this view in the following section.

What Has Been the Role of Financialization in Changing Inequality?

Financialization is a clumsy name for an ongoing shift in the authority over economic activity from national governments to financial actors—for the rise in power of the banks, and for the international integration of financial markets.

A common pattern in inequality measures around the world is the influence on the overall measure of inequality of increasing (and sometimes decreasing) incomes in the financial sector. This is hard to detect in survey data, which usually do not identify respondents according to whether they work in or out of finance. But it emerges very clearly when the between-groups component of a Theil index is calculated across sector categories, if (as is usually the case in national

---

1. This author's father, the economist John Kenneth Galbraith, used to call this "Galbraith's Law."

data sets) one of the included categories happens to be finance. In such data sets, one can read the effect of rising (and sometimes falling) incomes in finance directly from a table or chart. Or, it is often possible to infer the increasing importance of finance from geographic data sets, since most countries and regions have a "financial capital" where the bulk of incomes from that sector are reported. New York and London play that role in the West; Shanghai plays it in China; Moscow plays it in Russia, Sao Paulo in Brazil.

The financial sector influences inequalities in a second way, by concentrating the growth of investment, and therefore of the associated incomes, in a small quadrant of economic activity at any one time. This is a consequence of the herd mentality. At a particular moment, some sector becomes "hot" and all of the financial players rush for a "piece of the action." Some will succeed; many will fail. And there will be a penumbra of shady and fraudulent players, who (if left unchecked) may bring major risks to the stability of the system. But the effect on inequality stems from the initial rush, which must inevitably concentrate resources into the hands of "superstars"—for a short time. In contrast, typical public-sector financing of the economy spreads activity around; that is the nature of politics. The gains are smaller but more widely shared, the durability may be greater, and inequality is much less likely to increase.

What Do Global Patterns Show?

Looking at global patterns of changing inequality is another way to illustrate the modern power of global finance. A study conducted on the UTIP data set analyzed the general tendency for inequality to change, year by year from the early 1960s forward. Until 1971, there was no general tendency that could easily be seen. Some countries showed rising inequality, others showed falling inequality, and a reasonable observer might conclude that differences in national policies were the main factors.

From 1971 until around 1980, overall, inequality in the world declined, with the narrow (but important) exception of the recession-riddled industrial West, where it started to rise. Declines were especially sharp in a band of countries extending from Iran to Iraq and across North Africa to Algeria—a group clearly tied together by their common role as producers of oil. But other commodity producers also did well, as did the debt-fueled developing countries in the southern cone of South America.

And in 1981, things changed again. Inequality started rising as a dramatic, general pattern almost everywhere. Inequality rose most sharply at first in Latin America and Africa, the epicenters of the world debt crisis. Only those countries that had remained aloof from commercial bank financing were immune: China, India, and Iran. In the 1990s, the center of rapidly rising inequality shifted to Eastern Europe and the former Soviet Union; and in the later 1990s it moved on to Asia, and notably to liberalizing India and to China. Here again, there was an exception: the foreign direct investment-powered "Tigers" of Southeast Asia, until the crisis that hit them in 1997.

What was going on emerges with striking clarity from this picture. In the year 1971, the stabilizing global financial framework created at Bretton Woods in 1944 collapsed. There followed an oil-and-commodity boom that reduced inequalities in the producing countries and increased them among the consumers. Then, in the 1980s, ultra-high interest rates and rolling debt crises reversed the balance of financial power. This now unquestionably favored the rich and crushed the poor, first in Latin America and Africa, then in the communist states, and finally in Asia.

From this pattern the power of global financial forces is evident. Only those countries that had avoided commercial international debt escaped the storm, and only for so long as they could or chose to maintain their independence. Their capacity to do that was very limited, in this era of globalization, neoliberalism, and what was called the "Washington consensus" for economic policy, namely to privatize, deregulate, open up to external competition, and cut public spending and taxes.

But then, in 2000, the wheel turned one more time. Thanks to the bursting of the stock market bubble in the United States and in the wake of the 9/11 attacks, interest rates were cut practically to zero. Commodity prices rose worldwide, especially oil. China continued to grow, providing a new source of demand to many peripheral producers. In much of South America, Russia, and eventually even China itself, inequality peaked and began to decline, even as these regions took their distance from the neoliberal consensus of the 1990s and from the international institutions that enforced it. This phenomenon again confirms the importance of common global forces, while suggesting that even under "capitalism"—provided the policies are not too savage—there is no necessary tendency for inequality to increase forever. Inequalities may or may not increase, depending on world conditions that are set, to a great extent though not exclusively, by the powers that control world financial systems.

Estimated Gross Household Income Inequality, Decade by Decade Averages

These maps (Figure 7.2) show the decade-by-decade averages of the EHII data set, for the 1970s and the early 2000s. Note the clear pattern of lower inequality in richer countries (apart from China at the time) and the shift toward higher average inequality values. The lowest inequalities today are shown in Scandinavia; the erstwhile low values for the United Kingdom, France, Central Europe, Canada, Australia, and China have all disappeared.[2]

2. The maps were prepared by Aleksandra Malinowska.

Changes in Pay Inequalities: Selected Periods

The maps in Figures 7.3 to 7.6 show the annual percentage change in measures of *pay* inequality across industrial sectors, calculated from the UTIP-UNIDO data set, which is based directly on UNIDO's Industrial Statistics, over selected six-year intervals. The pay data set is the raw material from which estimated household income inequalities were computed, so the two measures are very close. But there are more observations in the pay data, and they change more over time, so it is easier to use them to pick up some of the dramatic shifts in inequality that occurred at particular moments, in particular at the time of the oil boom in the 1970s, the debt crisis of the 1980s, and when the Soviet Union disbanded in the 1990s. An interesting feature of this data shows up in the final map (Figure 7.6): a worldwide tendency for inequalities to *decline*, although from high levels, in the early part of the 2000s.

Oil Boom and Oil Shock

Notice the declines in producing countries (Algeria, Libya, Iraq, Iran) and the increases among importers, notably India and the United States (Figure 7.3).

Debt Crisis in the Third World

Note the increasing inequality in most countries of South America, Africa, and Asia (Figure 7.4). Chile is only an apparent exception; that country had already experienced sharply rising inequality following the 1973 coup, and in the banking crisis year of 1982—similarly for Bolivia. In the United States, industrial pay inequalities also rose sharply in the late 1970s and in the early 1980s recessions; the peak for that period was in 1982, and pay inequalities declined slightly with economic recovery after 1983.

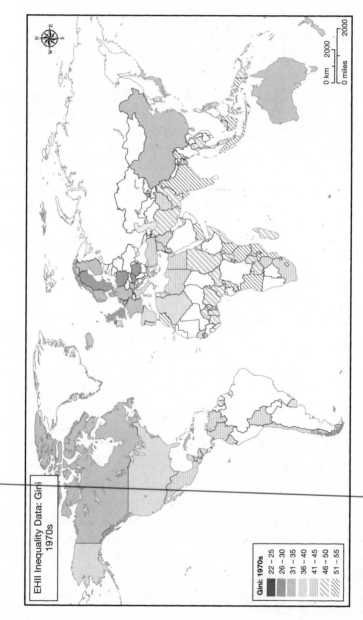

Figure 7.2 Estimated Inequality by Decades, 1970s and Early 2000s

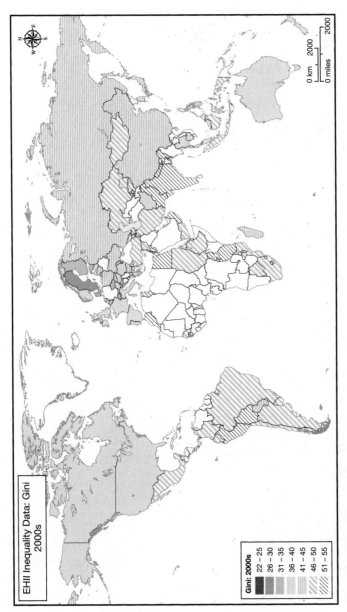

Figure 7.2 (Continud.)

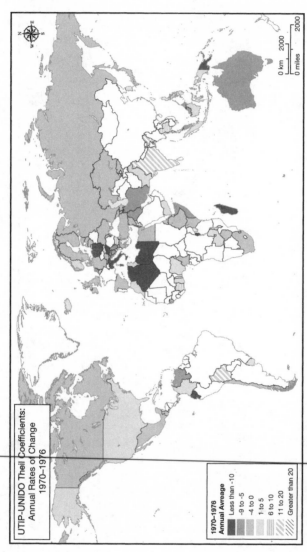

1) For the countries of the former USSR (Azerbaijan, Armenia, Estonia, Georgia, Kazakhstan, Kyrgyzstan, Latvia, Lithuania, Moldova, and Ukraine) data for the USSR were substituted for the years before the breakup.

2) For the countries of former Yugoslavia (Bosnia and Herzegovina, Croatia, Slovenia, The former Yugoslavic Republic of Macedonia, Serbia, and Montenegro) data for Yugoslavia were substituted for the years before the breakup.

3) For Slovakia, data before 1990 are filled in from Czechoslovakia, since Slovakia only became a country in 1993.

Figure 7.3 Change in Pay Inequality, 1970–1976

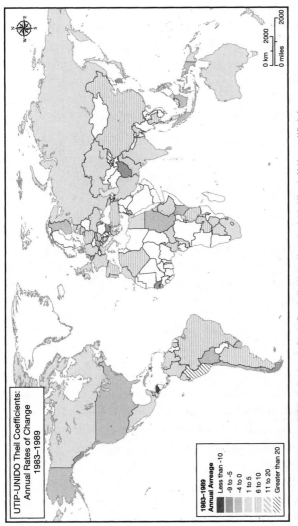

Figure 7.4 Change in Pay Inequality, 1983–1989

The End of the Communist Era and the Catastrophe of "Transition"

The dramatic collapse of the Soviet Union and of the regimes in its neighbors speaks for itself (Figure 7.5). Again note the declining pay inequality in the United States, as the information-technology boom got underway and the economy moved toward full employment. In the US case, pay inequalities fell, even though income inequalities rose to an unprecedented peak.

The Early 2000s: A Decade of Declining Inequalities

Note the declines in Russia, China, India, Indonesia, and much of Europe as well. The United States, once again in difficulties, shows rising industrial pay inequality in this period (Figure 7.6). In Brazil, pay inequalities seem to have risen, even though overall income inequalities tended to decline, quite sharply, after 2002. I have not inspected the case of New Zealand, a country that moved from a social-democratic model to free-market neoliberalism in the 1980s, and did not back off in the first decade of the 2000s, as did South Africa and parts of South America.

Conclusions

We have taken a quick tour of a large world, in search of regularities in the movement of economic inequality, so far as it can be observed through the lens of a large, consistent data set. The following general conclusions appear to be in order.

First, when analyzed with reliable world data, Kuznets's core insight remains valid. There is a trajectory of inequality in the course of economic development, structural change, and rising income. For most countries in the world today, growth reduces inequality and rich countries are more egalitarian than the poor. However, there are exceptions, notably at the low end of the scale—the rise of China, at least until recently, was accompanied by sharply rising inequality. And at the high

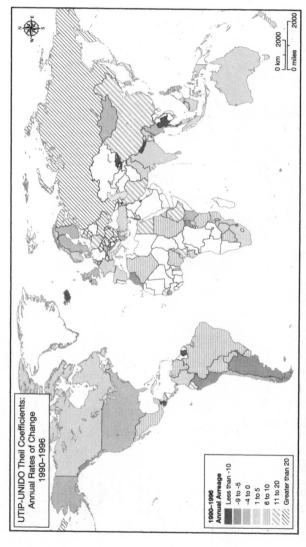

1) For the countries of the former USSR (Azerbaijan, Armenia, Estonia, Georgia, Kazakhstan, Kyrgyzstan, Latvia, Lithuania, Moldova, and Ukraine) data for the USSR were substituted for the years before the breakup.

2) For the countries of former Yugoslavia (Bosnia and Herzegovina, Croatia, Slovenia, The former Yugoslavic Republic of Macedonia, Serbia, and Montenegro) data for Yugoslavia were substituted for the years before the breakup.

3) For Slovakia, data before 1990 are filled in from Czechoslovakia, since Slovakia only became a country in 1993.

Figure 7.5 Change in Pay Inequality, 1990–1996

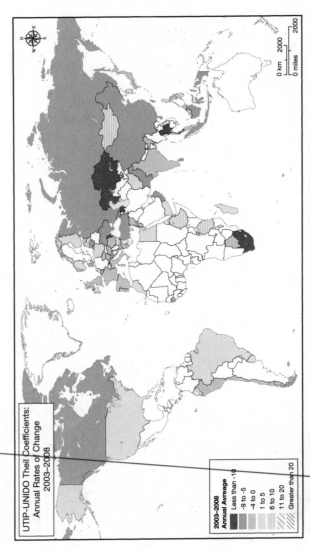

UTIP-UNIDO Theil Coefficients:
Annual Rates of Change
2003–2008

2003–2008
Annual Avreage
Less than -10
-9 to -5
-4 to 0
1 to 5
6 to 10
11 to 20
Greater than 20

1) For the countries of the former USSR (Azerbaijan, Armenia, Estonia, Georgia, Kazakhstan, Kyrgyzstan, Latvia, Lithuania, Moldova, and Ukraine)
data for the USSR were substituted for the years before the breakup.

2) For the countries of former Yugoslavia (Bosnia and Herzegovina, Croatia, Slovenia, The former Yugoslavic Republic of Macedonia, Serbia, and
Montenegro) data for Yugoslavia were substituted for the years before the breakup.

3) For Slovakia, data before 1990 are filled in from Czechoslovakia, since Slovakia only became a country in 1993.

Figure 7.6 Change in Pay Inequality 2003–2008

end, as technology and finance emanate from a few of the richest countries to the entire world, the Kuznets curve appears once again to turn up.

Second, political institutions have been and in some cases remain a bulwark against rising inequalities. When they crumble, the associated violence can contribute to abrupt changes, which may be difficult to reverse. Rising inequalities can happen quite suddenly, whereas—with just a few revolutionary exceptions—reducing them is a matter of patient progress over the years.

Third, global financial forces and changing financial conditions have played a powerful role affecting economic inequalities around the world over the past fifty years, especially since the breakup of the stabilizing framework of Bretton Woods in 1971.

Fourth, when we look at a large group of countries spanning the entire world, there appears to be no single permanent trend to inequality, neither down (as Kuznets surmised for the long run) nor up (as Piketty argues from a much smaller group). Instead, the great swing upward of income inequalities appears to have been mostly a phenomenon of the years from 1980 to 2000. After 2000, the trend stops, and though inequalities remained high, there was a tendency for them to decline in numerous widely separated countries. In South America, most notably, inequality and also poverty declined in many countries, including Brazil and Argentina, following crises that forced or enabled policy changes. Lower interest rates and better commodity prices appear to have been strong factors, as well as a retreat in many places from the free-market orthodoxies of the prior two decades.

8

ARE WE HEADING BACK TO THE VICTORIAN AGE?

In his important book published in 2014, *Capital in the Twenty-first Century*, Thomas Piketty of the Paris School of Economics has argued that, as a matter of fundamental tendency, capitalist systems produce rising inequalities in income and especially in wealth.[1] Piketty's fundamental argument rests on a simple inequality:

$$r > g$$

where r represents the rate of return on financial wealth, or what Piketty calls *capital*, and g represents the growth rate of the economy. So long as this inequality holds, Piketty argues, there is a tendency for wealth to concentrate and for inequality to rise. And, he argues, such a tendency is a deep feature of capitalism, which has largely held throughout history.

What Is "Capital"?

Piketty's book was marketed in the United States with the word "Capital" printed in large red letters on the cover, on a

1. This chapter is adapted from my review, *Kapital in the 21st Century?*, published in *Dissent*.

white background. The title thus invites a discussion of the meaning of this fraught and controversial concept.

The original *Capital*, or *Das Kapital*, first appeared in 1867. To Karl Marx, capital was a social, political, and legal category—the means of control of the means of production by the dominant class. Capital could be money, it could be machines; it could be fixed and it could be variable. But the essence of capital was neither physical nor financial. It was the power that capital gave to capitalists, namely the authority to make decisions and to extract surplus from the worker. It was thus the power to generate inequality. And for Marx, the fundamental division in society was between those who owned capital, and those who did not—who were, by that fact, obliged to sell their labor to those who did.

Early in the last century, neoclassical economics dumped this social and political analysis for a mechanical one. *Capital* was reframed as a physical item, which paired with labor to produce output. This notion of capital permitted mathematical expression of the "production function," so that wages and profits could be linked to the respective "marginal products" of each factor. The new vision thus raised the uses of machinery over the social role of its owners and legitimated profit as the just return for an indispensable contribution. Neoclassical economists thus treat the ratio of capital to income, K/Y, as a physical or technical relationship, connected to the productivity and efficiency of the capital stock.

Piketty's own approach to counting capital is in two parts. First, he conflates physical capital equipment with *all* forms of money-valued wealth, including land and housing, whether that wealth is in productive use or not. He excludes only what neoclassical economists call "human capital," presumably because it can't be bought and sold. Then he estimates the market value of that wealth. Thus although Piketty often speaks of capital, and of the movement of K/Y, as though physical quantities were changing, his notion of capital is not a physical but a money measure.[2]

So What Happened to "Capital" in the Twentieth Century?

The decline of Piketty's capital/income ratio in the early years of the twentieth century was mainly due to much higher incomes, produced by wartime mobilization, against the existing market capitalization, whose gains were restricted during the First World War. (In some countries, stock markets were simply closed.) Later, when asset values collapsed at the start the Great Depression, it wasn't physical capital that disintegrated, only its market value. And then came a new round of income gains (especially in the United States) in the Second World War, while capital gains were again held in check. All of these were mainly matters of financial valuation and money incomes, not physical investment or disinvestment. All of them, however, pushed Piketty's K/Y ratio down.

Piketty then goes on to show that in relation to current income, the market value of capital assets has risen sharply since the 1970s. In the Anglo-American world, he calculates, this ratio rose from 250–300 percent of income at that time to 500–600 percent today. In some sense, "capital" has once again become more important, more dominant, a bigger factor in economic life. Again, this is financial capital, not physical capital. And here is where Piketty starts to offer a general theory of the distribution of income.

2. For example, when Piketty describes the capital/income ratio plummeting in France, Britain, and the United States after 1910, he refers to wartime physical destruction of capital equipment. Yet obviously there was no physical destruction to speak of in Britain and none at all in the United States during the First World War—and that in France was vastly overstated, as Keynes showed in 1919. Belgium was another story, but Belgium is not one of the countries Piketty studies.

What Are Piketty's Fundamental Laws of Distribution?

Piketty attributes the rise in K/Y to slower economic growth in relation to the return on capital, according to the formula that he dubs a "fundamental law": $r > g$. Piketty argues that capitalism has a structural tendency for r to exceed g, hence for inequality to rise, because the ownership of capital is concentrated in the hands of relatively few people.

Where does the rate of return come from? Piketty never says. He merely asserts that the return on capital has usually averaged a certain value, say 5 percent on land in the nineteenth century, and higher in the twentieth. (There is a theory of the rate of return to *physical capital*, which Piketty sometimes endorses, but as we discussed earlier, it too is problematic.)

One problem here is that financial valuations may move in ways that may have nothing to do with "the rate of return." For instance, Piketty's capital-income ratio peaks for Japan in 1990—a quarter century ago, at the start of the long Japanese growth slump—and for the United States in 2008, at the start of the Great Financial Crisis, whereas in Canada, which did not have a financial crash, it was apparently still rising through 2012. A simple mind might say that market value is driven by financialization and exaggerated by bubbles, rising where they are permitted and falling when they pop. Such a theory would do a good job of explaining the fluctuations in the income distribution, especially in the United States, where income tax accounting captures reasonably well the actual incomes of the very rich.

Piketty contends that there is a long-run inexorable tendency for r to exceed g, producing rising inequality. But there are two reasons that this may not be so. First, taxation of interest income materially reduces the difference between r and g. Second, consumption out of interest income can reduce the extent to which financial balances build up over time. If profits are taxed and also consumed, they cannot also be accumulated and passed along.

Piketty's second fundamental law concerns the effect of savings on financial wealth. The key idea is that a high savings rate by wealthier people compounds their advantage and grows their incomes more rapidly than those who do not save. This law is subject to the same general criticism as the first: while it is true that you accumulate more by saving than by not saving, it is also true that taxes and inflation can deflate the value of accumulated wealth in relation to new income, and in practice they often have. History is littered with examples of deflated and exhausted fortunes—fortunately.

What Do Piketty's Data Show?

The empirical core of Piketty's book is about the distribution of income as revealed by tax records in a handful of rich countries—mainly France and Britain, but also the United States, Canada, Germany, Japan, Sweden, and some others. Its virtues lie in permitting a long view and in giving detailed attention to the income of elite groups, which other approaches to distribution often miss.

Piketty shows that in the mid-twentieth century the *income* share accruing to the top-most groups in his countries fell, beginning in the years after 1910. After 1945, the top shares remained low for three decades. They then rose from the 1980s onward, sharply in the United States and Britain and less so in Europe or Japan.

Thus the greater part of the twentieth century, at least from 1914 to 1980, stands as an exception to his law. Piketty attributes this in part to the world wars, but this is also the era when income taxation came into widespread use, while interest rates came under the control of central banks. Moreover, the indirect effect of the wars and associated social transformations included unionization and rising wages, progressive income tax rates, and postwar nationalizations and expropriations in Britain and France. During this period, r (after taxes) did *not* exceed g, and income inequality did not rise, in the countries that form the core of Piketty's own data. The assertion of a "long-run tendency" requires one to believe that the conditions of the nineteenth century and earlier will now return on a sustained basis.

Wealth concentrations seem to have peaked around 1910, fallen until 1970, and then increased once again. If Piketty's estimates are correct, top wealth shares in France and the United States remain today below their Belle Époque values, while US top income shares have returned to their values in the Gilded Age. Piketty also believes that the United States is an extreme case, that income inequality here today exceeds that in some major developing countries, including India, China, and Indonesia. We can see from the Appendix that other measures do not support this view.

But even within the United States there are reasons to be careful. Consider this (now famous) picture of the top-income share in US tax data, from Piketty's book (Figure 8.1). There are two sharp shifts in the data: one in the early 1940s and the other (much smaller) in the late 1980s. The first one coincides with the outbreak of the Second World War, at which time top tax rates

The top decile share in U.S. national income dropped from 45–50% in the 1910s–1920s
to less than 35% in the 1950s (this is the fall documented by Kuznets);
it then rose from less than 35% in the 1970s to 45–50% in the 2000s–2010s.

Figure 8.1 Share of Top Decile in US Income, 1910–2012.

Source: Piketty, *Capital in the 21st Century*, p. 24.

were raised to very high levels (92 percent)—precisely in order to discourage "war millionaires." This was obviously effective, although it may also have encouraged companies to reward their execs in ways that did not show up on tax filings.

And on the other hand, in 1986, Congress enacted the Tax Reform Act of 1986, which lowered top tax rates and broadened the base of taxable incomes. This would have the effect of increasing measured top incomes—but obviously those incomes were present beforehand. No underlying change in the economy paralleled the tax and reporting change, and thus the upward shift in the top share right after 1986 is an exaggeration.

Under President Reagan, changes to US tax law also encouraged higher pay to corporate executives, the use of stock options, and (indirectly) the splitting of new technology firms into separately capitalized enterprises, which would eventually include Intel, Apple, Oracle, Microsoft, and the rest. Now, top incomes are no longer fixed salaries but instead closely track the stock market. This is the simple result of concentrated ownership, the flux in asset prices, and the use of capital funds for executive pay. This shows up in the two peaks of the Piketty graph, at the peak of the NASDAQ boom in 2000, and at the peak of the real estate debacle in 2007.[3]

Are We Heading Back to the Nineteenth Century?

The movement toward a high top income share in the Piketty graph certainly looks ominous. It is worth noting, however, that it measures top incomes over a century in a society that changed radically during that time, and in ways not reflected in

3. Travis Hale and I documented the correspondence of high incomes in the late 1990s to the information-technology boom in a paper back in 2004. See *Working Paper 27* at http://utip.gov.utexas.edu.

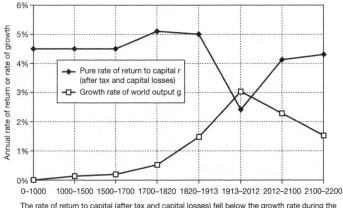

The rate of return to capital (after tax and capital losses) fell below the growth rate during the 20th century, and might again surpass it in the 21st century.

Figure 8.2 The after-tax rate of return on capital and the growth rate, as presented by Piketty for the years 0 to 2200.

Source: Piketty, Capital in the 21st Century, p. 357.

the figure. For instance, in 1929, when the top share reached its early peak, there was no Social Security, no unemployment insurance, no Medicare, Medicaid, Food Stamps, or Earned Income Tax Credit, no secondary mortgage market—in fact, none of the institutions that created the modern middle class in America existed. In the 1980s, when top shares rose again, they did so in a much richer, and also much more middle-class society. The institutions make a difference—and continue to do so—so that the peak of 2000 cannot truly be compared to the peak of 1929.

In certain other respects, it also seems that Piketty overstates his claim. For instance, here is a chart (Figure 8.2) that he uses to buttress the claim that $r > g$ (and therefore rising inequality) is the normal state of the world, to which we are destined to return. But notice that the "data" start way back in year zero (!) and that they continue out to year 2200 (!!). Notice also that the exception—the years of the twentieth century, are reduced to a single point, so that the figure shows a clear return to the long-term pattern of the distant past.

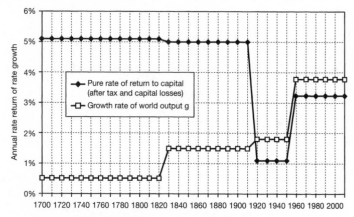

The rate of return to capital (after tax and capital losses) fell below the growth rate during the 20th century, and may again surpass it in the 21st century.

Figure 8.3 AThe after-tax rate of return on capital and the growth rate: actual data and undistorted time scale.

Source: Noah Wright. Used with permission.

But of course the early years are speculative, and the later (future) ones are only projections. Here is what the chart would look like if we show only the years from 1700 to the present for which Piketty presents more-or-less documented facts, and if we present the years in proportion to their actual length (Figure 8.3). Clearly, this chart—and so the real evidence—does *not* support the notion that *r > g* is "normal." And it does not tell us anything about what may be likely to happen next.[4]

Why Is Piketty's Study of Financial Valuations Interesting?

As Adam Smith argued, private financial valuation measures power, including political power, even if the holder plays no

4. For a complete set of charts showing the visual distortions in Piketty's work, see Noah Wright, "Data Visualization in Piketty's Capital in the 21st Century," *UTIP Working Paper No. 70.*

active economic role. Absentee landlords and the Koch brothers have power of this type. Piketty calls it "patrimonial capitalism"—in other words, not the real thing, but an important phenomenon in a system of social and political control by those who have financial wealth.

Thanks to the French Revolution, registry of wealth and inheritance has been good in Piketty's homeland for a long time. This allows Piketty to show how the simple determinants of the concentration of wealth are the rate of return on assets and the rates of economic and population growth. If the rate of return exceeds the growth rate, then the rich and the elderly gain in relation to everyone else. Meanwhile, inheritances depend on the extent to which the elderly accumulate—which is greater the longer they live—and on the rate at which they die. These two forces yield a flow of inheritances that Piketty estimates to be about 15 percent of annual income presently in France—astonishingly high for a factor that gets no attention at all in newspapers or textbooks.

Moreover, for France, Germany, and Britain, the "inheritance flow" has been rising since 1980, from negligible levels to substantial ones, due to a higher rate of return on financial assets along with a slightly rising mortality rate in an older population. The trend seems likely to continue—though one wonders about the effect of the financial crisis on valuations. Piketty also shows (to the small extent that data allow) that the share of global wealth held by a tiny group of billionaires has been rising much more rapidly than average global income.

So How about a Global Tax on Wealth?

Piketty writes:

> no matter how justified inequalities of wealth may be initially, fortunes can grow and perpetuate themselves beyond all reasonable limits and beyond any

possible rational justification in terms of social utility. Entrepreneurs thus tend to turn into rentiers, not only with the passing of generations but even within a single lifetime. . . . [A] person who has good ideas at the age of forty will not necessarily still be having them at ninety, nor are his children sure to have any. Yet the wealth remains. . . .

With this passage he makes a distinction that he previously blurred: between wealth justified by "social utility" and the other kind. It is, in part, the old distinction between "profit" and "rent." Recall that as far back as Ricardo, classical economists called for taxation to fall on rent, which had no social utility, and to exempt profit, which did.

Piketty's own remedy is a dramatic call for a "progressive global tax on capital"—by which he means a wealth tax. Indeed, what could be better suited to an age of inequality (and budget deficits) than a levy on the holdings of the rich, wherever and in whatever form they may be found? But if such a tax fails to discriminate between fortunes that have ongoing "social utility" and those that don't—a distinction Piketty himself has just drawn—then it may not be the most carefully thought-out idea. We shall have a bit more to say on this in the chapter devoted to wealth.

9

NORMS AND CONSEQUENCES

The economies of almost all nation-states have experienced significant increases in economic inequality over the past generation, so that with almost no exceptions the world's peoples belong to more unequal countries than they did in 1960 or even in 1980. Whether the same claim applies to the world's population as a whole is less certain: in 1960 the gap in living standards between (let's say) Europe and China was much larger than it is today. However, any claim about the inequality of the world's population taken as a single unit depends on comparisons of national living habits and price levels, and so rests on a much less firm foundation than analyses of developments within individual countries. And for most people, it is the comparison with compatriots that matters.

What then are the consequences of higher and rising inequality? What effects can be discerned or discovered? That is the topic of the present chapter.

Does Inequality Help or Hurt Economic Growth?

Perhaps the most commonly raised concern about economic inequality is that it may have an adverse effect on economic growth. This is, however, not the only possible view.

As we saw back in Chapter 2, the young John Maynard Keynes believed that the great inequalities of the nineteenth century were—in Britain at least—a fundamental ingredient of that country's economic expansion and of its dominance in the world at that time. The reason was that the rich of newly industrial Britain understood instinctively that their position depended on the moral use of their wealth—that they should save and invest it, and not fritter it away in frivolous enjoyments. Victorian virtue consisted in thrift on one side, and industry on the other.

A modern version of the Victorian story underpinned the "supply-side economics" of the Reagan Revolution, under which reduced taxation was supposed to generate increases in "saving, investment and work effort." An international version of this thesis has been presented more recently by a number of authors, notably Kristin Forbes of MIT in an influential 2000 article. Forbes argued that as a general rule, a rise of inequality would lead to concentrated saving and investment activity, followed by a surge of economic growth. She presented evidence based on the DS data set—perhaps the best available at that time. However, it is fair now to say that the evidence presented then was far from persuasive.

The opposite view is associated with Nancy Birdsall of the Center for Global Development and her co-authors. Their thesis holds that greater equality is associated with stronger growth, mainly because a more egalitarian society creates stronger incentives to develop education, training, and job skills. The case in point for the Birdsall thesis is the rise (especially in the 1990s) of relatively egalitarian Asian societies, such as Korea and Taiwan, on the strength of intensive efforts to foster human development. And indeed if one looks at a selection of Asian countries in the 1990s, it does appear that the more egalitarian ones had stronger rates of growth.

For egalitarians, the Birdsall view is intrinsically more attractive than the Forbes view. But can either be correct in the long run?

To see the problem, consider the following statement: "the position of the accelerator determines the speed of the car."

Is it true? You might say, "Of course! When the accelerator is down, the car speeds up." But think again, is this always true? Of course not. The car must be in working order, it must have fuel, it must be turned on, it must be in gear, it must be on a surface that can be driven. And even if all those conditions are met, and the car does speed up, the effect cannot last long. Cars have a maximum speed; they run out of gas, and in the long run, whatever else happens, they slow down and stop. For this reason, no statistical correlation of accelerator *position* with *speed* will be correct, if all the cars in all their conditions are being measured.

To put the point another way, suppose it were true that low inequality were associated with higher growth. In that case, after a certain amount of time, the low-inequality countries would all be rich, and the high-inequality countries would all be poor. Now, it is true that the rich countries tend to have lower inequality than the poor ones. But it does not follow that they started out that way! And in fact, we know that they did not. The Kuznets thesis tells us that an egalitarian system is something won, partly in the course of development and partly by social and political struggle along the way.

Conversely, suppose it were true that high levels of inequality systematically produced higher growth. In that case, after a certain amount of time, the rich countries would be highly unequal and the egalitarian countries would be poor! But again we know this is not the case. It is true that some of the most egalitarian countries—the communist states—failed to maintain the growth and development they required in order to stay in competition with the capitalist West. But within the West, it was those countries that were the most egalitarian that have become the wealthiest of all, thanks to high levels of investment and productivity growth. Therefore, and regardless of any regression result, it cannot be true that concentrating income and wealth confers a decisive advantage in economic growth.

How Is Inequality Related to Poverty, Health, and Happiness?

At first glance, the relationship between inequality and poverty may seem obvious. A more egalitarian society will have fewer poor than a less equal society at the same income level. It cannot be otherwise; the very definition of greater equality is that fewer people will be found at far removes from the center of the distribution.

Yet it is not quite so simple. Many economists have for many years accepted the notion that "efficiency" and "equity" are competing claims, and that if one pursues equity in terms of a more egalitarian society as a political value, one must incur a cost in terms of total income and living standards. If so, it should be possible for an egalitarian society to be entirely composed of the poor.

A striking fact revealed by the EHII data set is that there seems to exist no such society in the world. Egalitarian states are almost all rich; poor countries are all highly unequal. The one *possible* extant exception in the world today is Cuba. But in the Cuban case, the question of how income should be measured is a very difficult one. It is true that in terms of material goods and housing, Cubans live at a low standard compared to the "advanced" countries. But on the other hand, Cuban levels of education, health, professional development, and life expectancy are high, comparable with countries that enjoy much higher personal living standards. Which of these factors should count more, in judging what is, actually, the Cuban "level of income"? There is no good answer to that question.

The epidemiologists Richard Wilkinson and Kate Pickett have analyzed health, mortality, life expectancy, and other factors and have made a striking generalization: that egalitarian societies do better in these terms. The insight behind this finding has its roots in studies of bureaucratic structures; in earlier studies Wilkinson found that in the British civil service, those lower in the status hierarchy have greater health problems than those who rise to the top. The stress of being stuck in an inferior position would appear to be a major force in that situation. The Wilkinson-Pickett joint work extends this basic finding to a substantial number of inter-country comparisons.

Wilkinson and Pickett's work has attracted criticism, especially allegations that their statistical results are governed by special cases ("outliers") and that they may have disregarded countries that did not fall close to the lines of correlation that they report. More fundamentally, it is worth asking whether it is plausible that the citizens of a large country, like France or Germany or the United States, really spend their time comparing themselves to the richest and poorest citizens of their land—from whom they may be geographically and socially entirely remote. Perhaps they only compare themselves to neighbors, colleagues, and family members? If so, there would be no reason to expect a national measure of inequality, however accurate, to be a good index of the stress affecting any given person. If, on the other hand, people compare themselves to what they see on television, a different answer would follow.

Next, there is the question of whether citizens of more equal lands are happier—in some sense, and after controlling for income levels—than the denizens of unequal places. It seems reasonably well accepted that happiness rises with income, up to a certain (modest) level, and that further gains in national income beyond that level have no detectable effect on national psychological well-being.

But does *equality* improve happiness? Should it? Frankly, this author has no earthly idea.

How Is Inequality Related to Unemployment?

A more fruitful line of inquiry concerns the relationship between inequalities of pay and rates of unemployment. Here there are two sharply contrasting theoretical positions, with major policy implications around the world.

One line of argument is rooted in the conventional supply-and-demand framework of the labor market. It holds that the drive of workers for higher (and more equal) wages, whether advanced through unions or minimum wage laws or fair labor standards, is a move toward rigidity in labor markets. And in the face of rapid technological change, in the course of which employers are seeking for more productive workers to whom they are willing to pay more, while less productive workers are increasingly worth less, a rigid labor market creates a "mismatch" between the supply of skills and the demand for them, and therefore is responsible for unemployment. In Europe, especially, this argument is often made to explain the large-scale mass unemployment in supposedly egalitarian European states, and to support calls for "labor market reform" that would reduce the power of unions and the rights of workers to tenure and benefits from their jobs.

A clear implication of this argument is that countries with less equal pay structures should enjoy less unemployment, and the comparison is often drawn between social-democratic "Europe" and the free-market United States in that regard.

However, there are at least two lines of well-accepted theory that run the other way. One of them is associated with two mainstream economists, John Harris and Michael Todaro, who examined pay differentials, migration, and unemployment in East Africa in the 1960s. They observed that in countries where the cities had a minimum wage, but the hinterland did not, people would move to the city in the hope of landing one of the (scarce) better-paid jobs. Since there were many people doing this and only a small number of jobs, the result was unemployment, hitherto unknown in those societies. Inequality, in other words, breeds unemployment.   ˻or the minimum wage

The Harris-Todaro model has broad application in the modern world, where long-distance migration and job search have become pervasive. In modern China a floating population of tens of millions from the countryside orbits the cities in search of jobs in construction and other trades. In modern Europe, long-distance migration across countries for job search has become routine; it is invariably from the poorer to the richer regions. The same holds for North America, where migration from Mexico and Central America to the United States and Canada has succeeded the massive migrations of rural African Americans from the Deep South to the industrial Midwest in the 1940s and 1950s.

Migration is not the only source of unemployment, but any major inequality in the pay structure will have a similar effect; people will leave low-paid jobs for a better statistical probability of landing a better one. They know that employers, as a general rule, like to hire the applicants who are on hand, not those who lack the motivation to seek them out. And conversely, in egalitarian societies, there is less incentive to quit low-productivity and low-paid jobs, simply because the income gains that are potentially available are not so dramatic. Egalitarian societies should therefore be, as a rule, more stable and they should enjoy less, not more, unemployment.

The evidence within Europe broadly supports the Harris-Todaro hypothesis: there is a strong statistical association between greater equality and lower unemployment, after controlling for other factors, including income level and the youth share in population. The egalitarian northern European countries have enjoyed consistently lower unemployment than their less-equal southern European countries, and certain small countries, notably Austria and Ireland, were able to enjoy low unemployment for substantial periods while pursuing strongly egalitarian and centralized internal wage structures.

But what about that comparison between "Europe" and the United States? Even there, it is not obvious that the standard story holds up. For comparisons with the United States invariably relate to income data, not pay, in which the greater inequality of the United States stems (as we have seen) from a strong element of concentrated capital-asset incomes.

And—more important—those comparisons have all been of the United States against individual European countries. It is true that the United States is much more unequal than most of them—for example, Denmark, or even Germany. But Europe is not a collection of separated countries any longer; it is a single integrated continental economy. If one measures inequalities of pay across Europe taken as a single entity, then it is necessary to count in the differences in average pay across countries—the large differences between (say) Germany and Poland or Norway and Romania. Once one does this, the picture changes, and in the available calculations, European pay inequality is *greater*, not less, than that in the United States. So, again, the historically better performance of the United States on the employment front is not a surprise.

There is a second theory linking egalitarian pay to good economic performance, which we take up in the next section.

How Is Inequality Related to Productivity Growth?

In the early 1950s two Swedish trade union economists, Rudolf Meidner and Gösta Rehn, formulated a theory of egalitarian wage structures that had been guiding Swedish social-democratic policy since the mid-1930s and that would continue to do so for another thirty years.

The Meidner-Rehn argument rested on the fact that in all industries and most other economic sectors as well, there is a spectrum of available degrees of efficiency and productivity, from best practice and progressive to retrograde and inferior. Naturally, the more productive a firm, the less labor it uses per unit of output and the higher the wages it can comfortably pay, and vice versa.

Therefore, they reasoned, wage policy should prohibit the payment of low wages, on the ground that this will force backward firms to upgrade, and will give progressive firms a strong competitive advantage. Over time, the more advanced firms will occupy a larger share of the national economy, the incorrigible reactionaries will be forced to the wall, and national productivity and living standards will improve. This process is compatible with open trade—indeed it cannot work under trade protections, and it requires only that the state actively retrain displaced workers and provide employment for those who cannot make it in the advanced sectors.

It may be argued that this "Scandinavian" or "LO" model played a powerful role in transforming Sweden from a country with roughly average income for Europe, strongly dependent on timber, iron, and other natural resources, into the engineering, aviation, and automotive powerhouse that it eventually became. However, one may question whether the principle can be made to work in a large country, which cannot so effectively transform all of its industries into world-beaters, but must accept a mix of the fully competitive and the merely average—and therefore a mix of high and lower wages.

How about a Biological Model?

One final model of inequality and economic performance bears mention, and that is the biological/anthropological approach pioneered by Thorstein Veblen and developed by the institutionalist school, including notably the white-collar criminologist William K. Black and also this author, in a 2008 book called *The Predator State*.

Veblen's idea (as we have seen in Chapter 2) was that human society is continuous with that of primitive or barbarian social formations, and even with the animal world. It consists, not of classes in conflict or cooperation, nor of bloodless "factors of production," but of quasi-separated worlds of "industry" and "exploit." The former is the world of work—dreary, irksome, necessary, and productive. The latter, which is descended from the hunt, is by nature *predatory*—it thrives at the expense of the productive or industrial sectors, and its dominance is imposed by force and fraud or by the force of law, expressed in personal property rights.

The concept of white-collar fraud is not well developed in economics; most economists have assumed that fraud cannot be an important force because markets will screen it out. Black contributes the concept of *control fraud*, which is the illegal extraction of wealth from a company by its own top executives—a concept also known as looting. The specific markers of control fraud are rapid corporate growth, high stock market valuations, too-good-to-be-true business plans and reporting, and vast accumulations of personal wealth by the insiders. Control frauds always fail in the end—but their consequence is to allow small numbers to accumulate great wealth, increasing inequality. This was the dominant feature of the Savings and Loan crisis in the United States in the 1980s; it played an important role in parts of the information-technology boom in the late 1990s; it was the signature of such firms as Enron, Tyco, and Worldcom in the early 2000s; and it was the key characteristic of the entire financial sector, from mortgage originations to ratings to securitization to phony foreclosures, in the housing finance disaster that produced the Great Financial Crisis of 2007–2009. The very language of that era—"liars loans," "neutron loans," and "toxic waste" are just a few examples—bespeaks the corruption of the system.

A central contribution of *The Predator State* concerns the role of public programs and institutions created during the twentieth century, in the United States mainly by the New Deal of Franklin Roosevelt and the Great Society of Lyndon Johnson. Three of these are Social Security, Medicare, and Medicaid, each of which today is a powerful source of income, counter-cyclical stabilization, and economic activity—and all the more so as the population ages and as manufacturing moves to other locations in the world. As these events unfolded, it became clear to certain parties that the public programs, including health care and education systems, were not peripheral to the economy; they had become its central structures, and also presented tempting targets for the extraction of wealth. The phenomenon of a predator state consists of private interests that arrive in public office, and that then conduct concerted efforts to skim substantial resources from these (and other) public programs, for example by privatizing public pensions, or by providing pharmaceutical insurance to seniors while pumping extraordinary sums into the pockets of pharmaceutical providers. These activities are also, in part, responsible for rising inequalities, and at the same time, high inequalities create the political conditions under which they can thrive.

Should Inequality Be Controlled?

In brief summary, the evidence does not permit one to say that inequality is either good or bad for growth, and it may or may not be correct to argue that more equal societies are healthier, longer-lived, and happier, at least above a certain income level. But there is compelling evidence that, within reasonable limits, lower degrees of inequality foster improved economic performance, and that rising inequality is a sign of trouble to come.

In particular, there is strong evidence that egalitarian wage structures foster lower unemployment and make migrations less attractive. For smaller countries, where external trade is a large part of the picture, there is good reason to believe that egalitarian structures can foster productivity growth and an improved competitive position if they are accompanied by open trade and active labor market policies with respect to education, training, and job placement. Finally, one may reasonably regard high inequality as posing large risks of control fraud and of generalized predation, where the instruments of state policy intended to support the vulnerable population get diverted to the further enrichment of a few. Rising inequality is the mark of a bubble, and bubbles are commonly infested with fraud.

Let me conclude this section by suggesting a biological analogy, useful perhaps in some situations. In the general run of middle- and upper-middle-class advanced countries, it seems, the measure of economic inequality is a bit like human blood pressure. There is a normal range that can be considered healthy; within that range, lower values are generally better. Inequality, like blood pressure, can be too low; the economic body then becomes sluggish and under-responsive. Zero inequality, like zero blood pressure, is for the morgue.

With rising inequality, there may be no immediate symptoms. Indeed the cause may be related to prosperity and to the excesses of prosperous times. But as inequality rises, there is trouble ahead; the chances of a major crisis increase. And a crisis, when it occurs, is not merely a "shock" or a "setback," leading to a "recession." It can be a life-threatening event, an economic heart attack or a stroke, inflicting damage that may be difficult to repair.

And that, above all, is a reason for concern and for monitoring the change of inequalities, just as doctors monitor the blood pressure of their patients—and for careful measures to keep inequalities from growing out of control.

10

POLICIES AGAINST
INEQUALITIES

We shall now take it as a point of departure that actual economic inequalities in many countries, including the United States, are excessive and should be reduced. Not all readers will agree, and although this author holds a definite view, it has not been a goal of this book to argue either side of the case. But a good survey of the issues requires us to describe the remedies most widely proposed, and for that purpose, in this chapter, we shall allow that there is a problem.

Policy discussions are often very specific to the history, laws, and institutions of a particular country, and the case of inequalities is no exception. While some of the issues discussed in this chapter can be treated in general and abstract terms, and as having reference to a wide range of nations, if not to all of them, we shall have recourse here mainly to the case of the United States. Readers from other countries may wish to consider how the principles involved may apply to the cases they know better.

Policies to reduce inequality of pay, income, and expenditure can be divided into three major types. There are, first of all, policies that affect the structure of pay and incomes, before taxes or government transfer programs come into play. These policies have their impact by raising the incomes of the poor, or by lowering the relative incomes of the rich. The second type consists of the effect on given incomes of tax and transfer programs. These policies have their impact by altering the private distribution of income after the fact—but before income is available to be used for private consumption or savings. A third type— much less discussed—also bears mention; these are policies that change the cost of living in ways that differently affect households at different income levels, for instance by taxing the sale of commodities or by providing low-cost public goods. Such policies make the distribution of post-tax, post-transfer income more or less effective in supporting an egalitarian community.

We shall take up the three types in turn.

Did Antitrust Policies Reduce Inequalities?

Antitrust was perhaps the first great egalitarian policy of the modern age, although dwarfed in moral significance in the nineteenth century by the abolition of slavery and by the Homestead Act, each of which conveyed property rights, in the self and in the land, to persons previously denied those rights.

The point of antitrust was straightforward: the Gilded Age was the age of trusts. Trusts were monopolies: industrial empires built and maintained for the benefit of a small plutocracy. Monopolies had been known, since the time of Adam Smith and even long before, to be an evil conducive to the accumulation of vast ill-got gains. The purpose of the antitrust laws was to dissolve those monopolies and to tame the economic power that they conferred.

Did it work? It's hard to find strong evidence that it did. John D. Rockefeller's Standard Oil was broken up, for example, but the Rockefeller family diversified, and continued to dominate the economic and political scene for many decades. Andrew Carnegie left no heirs, but a vast fortune. A considerable part of Andrew Mellon's fortune—the foundation of the National Gallery of Art, for instance—did come to the government in the end, but that was a tax case, rather than the consequence of antitrust. Antitrust is a tool to tame some of the worst abuses of corporate power; it does not prevent the concentration of private wealth.

Can Free Trade Reduce Inequalities?

When Adam Smith wrote about the inequalities that stemmed from the "policy of Europe," he had in mind monopolies granted by the state, the system of guilds and apprenticeships that prevented competition even between village craftsmen, and the general restriction on freedom of international trade. Many of those restrictions persist to this day, in licensing requirements and what is known to international trade negotiators as "intellectual property rights."

Over fifty years or so, the world has moved inexorably toward greater trade, and most observers would agree that the effect has been to increase inequalities in the wealthier countries, not to decrease them. The reason for this lies in the fact that the primary losers from free trade are the manufacturing workers in the low- and middle-technology industries of the advanced countries, from apparel and textiles to automobiles and heavy machinery. Since these workers formed (at one time) a good share of the industrial lower middle class, their displacement is a major factor in what observers have called the "disappearing middle" of the pay structure.

But is the trade that brings this about actually "free trade"? The answer on inspection is: obviously not. Free trade agreements are very long! They run thousands of pages. They are, in fact, detailed regulations for the *control* of trade and for the freedom of investment. Much of what they control, and seek to preserve, are the monopoly powers and privileges of particular corporations and professions, from technology companies to pharmaceutical makers to Hollywood movie studios, and from surgeons to therapists to lawyers. These powers and privileges are vested in patent, trademark, and copyright laws, and in licensing requirements, which their holders seek to enforce on the world marketplace.

The implication is that a system of truly free trade would reduce the monopoly profits, or economic rents, associated with being a US pharmaceutical giant or brain surgeon. Remove the rents, permit free competition in the industry or profession, and the inequality of incomes would have to decline. Similarly, reduction in copyright and patent protections would bring a reduction in the price of books, movies, and innovations, as the world would move quickly to copy and reproduce that which it found useful.

The premise of the argument, of course, is that the protections in question serve no useful function. And that is the fly in the soup. There are studies that show that in the case of pharmaceuticals, vast resources are devoted to innovation designed only to preserve and extend patent protections. But on the other hand, is every country equally capable of producing adequately trained medical personnel? Is the interoperability of every form of professional credential desirable, or would it destroy the ability of society to exercise control over the quality of the services it permits to be provided on its own territory? I do not have a general answer to this question.

Can the Financial Transactions Tax Reduce Inequalities?

In the 1970s the Yale economist James Tobin proposed a tax on financial transactions, and in particular on foreign exchange trades that were, at the time, thought to be a major source of instability in the value of the US dollar. Tobin's idea was to "throw sand in the gears" of the financial markets, by penalizing short-term speculations and encouraging investors to evade the tax by hanging on to their assets. A presumption, valid in the 1970s but much less so today, was that traders would be largely obliged to conduct transactions in their home markets, and that it would not be easy to evade the tax simply by relocating deals to untaxed venues, such as the Bahamas or the Cayman Islands.

Since then, the Tobin tax has become an iconic symbol for anti-inequality movements around the world, which have come to believe that it could serve as an effective way to generate revenue for international development aid and other good (and redistributive) causes. Even the conservative governments of some countries (notably, Germany) have endorsed the idea in principle—which may be a concession to popular opinion—or it may indicate their conclusion that the tax would not, in fact, raise much revenue or change the short-term culture of global finance by very much.

It seems true that the Tobin tax might have an important effect on one recent phenomenon in financial markets that cannot be outsourced, namely the creation of high-speed trading systems that effectively "front-run" ordinary investors by intercepting their orders to buy and sell. These systems require massive computer investments in proximity to the markets, as they rely on tiny differences in the time it takes electronic signals to move at close to the speed of light. These systems are purely predatory; rendering them unprofitable and shutting them down would be an excellent policy. However, the fortunes made from these systems accumulate in very few hands, and so the dent made in the overall structure of pay and income inequalities, while useful, would likely be quite small.

Can Unions and Minimum Wages Reduce Inequalities?

A much more broadly based policy approach is to focus on the wage incomes of the working population, on the theory that if these incomes are high and level, the larger society cannot remain highly unequal. An egalitarian working population would level economic outcomes on its own, and would generate political forces with egalitarian values, who could be counted on to rein in the excesses of the plutocracy that remains.

There are perhaps three basic ways to produce an egalitarian pay structure for the working population. The first is to foster widespread unionization, collective bargaining, and stable pay structures with differentials based mainly on seniority and credentials. The second is to legislate a high minimum wage, so that those without the benefit of a strong bargaining position have a basic level of wage protection. And the third—exercised over the years in a few countries, including Austria, Australia, and Ireland—is to have a national wage bargain, so as to assure a common pattern of shared wage gains and a more egalitarian distribution. Even in the United States, which relied in the 1950s and 1960s mainly on "pattern bargaining" led by the major trade unions in automobiles, steel, and rubber, there was a national policy in the 1960s of wage gains (after taking account of inflation) matched to the average and expected rate of productivity growth.

There is little doubt that countries with strong unions and high minimum wage laws—in relation to the average productivity of the country—have less inequality than those in the opposite position. The few countries with national wage bargains enjoyed among the lowest levels of inequality in relation to their levels of income, in the non-communist world. More broadly, unions support egalitarian social institutions in many different ways, including social insurance and other programs that benefit everyone. Weakening and breaking up unions, as happened in the United States from the late 1970s and early 1980s onward, is a reliable way to increase economic inequalities.

Can Education and Job Training Reduce Inequalities?

A widespread belief among economists, political figures, and the general public holds that investments in education will increase the supply of skills and will lower the "premium" associated with the acquisition of particular degrees of education. The result, if the principles of market economics apply to labor, wages, and the pricing of skills, should be a more egalitarian labor market.

One line of evidence often presented for this argument holds that the spread of high school education through the population in the first third of the twentieth century helped to produce the "Great Compression" in the structure of wages that characterized the second third of the century. However, most of the change actually occurred during the Second World War. In 1999 this author and Thomas Ferguson conducted a comprehensive decomposition of the sources of changing wages in the period from 1920 to 1947, and were able to assign over 90 percent of the variations to sources that had nothing to do with education or the supply of skills. We concluded:

> during World War Two, the enormous rise in wages of the truly unskilled workers who toiled in agriculture and on the public roads owed nothing to any Roads Scholarships program. The spectacular rise in their wages was the effect, surely, of demand, spurred by record public deficits, and the absorption of some ten million men into uniformed government employment. And the result was an almost perfect inversion of Protestant ideology and conventional thinking about education and labor markets, for the prime beneficiaries certainly included many millions of workers who were functionally illiterate and possessed of the very lowest educational credentials of all. It was this wage structure, socially constructed in national emergency though it was, that persisted for a generation following the war.

In more recent times, the claim that increasing education will diminish the wage and income advantages enjoyed by those at the top of the pay scale runs into two major difficulties. The first is that income advantages in the advanced sectors that dominate the increase in overall inequality in the United States are generally not due to wage payments at all, but to ownership rights in the companies and to the market valuation of those companies, that is, to their stock price. It is one thing to claim that the people who happen to *own* the shares of a company are, by some alchemy, also paragons of skill and genius—such claims are staples of tech-firm public relations—and quite a different thing to take that claim seriously as a matter of fact.

The other problem is that the supply-and-demand story of wage adjustment in response to excess supply seriously misstates the dynamic of employee compensation in the most advanced and therefore best-paid economic sectors. Firms in these areas are not engaged in routine manufacturing or service provision, where the question of wage costs is fundamental. They are, rather, engaged in a race to develop new products and techniques, so as to dominate a highly fluid and transient market for a short period of time. There is no question in these sectors of firms succeeding in this race by recruiting cheap employees, and equally no reason to believe that everyone who wishes to work in this area can find a job simply by lowering their wages. On the contrary: firms in these winner-take-all areas compete by paying top dollar to the best in the business, and the pay packets for those with such reputations will skyrocket, while the number of people actually employed remains small.

Under such a market structure, investing in education in an area requiring advanced skills, such as computer program design or electrical engineering, is not akin to growing apples or oranges for market. It is rather like buying lottery tickets: the payoff may be enormous, but only a fraction of those who take the gamble will see any benefit at all.

The structure of educational institutions in the United States also tends to belie the conventional formulation, under which "years of education" count as a proxy measure of "skill." The reality, as all Americans know, is that years of education are not meaningfully equivalent; the country has a steep hierarchy of academic institutions at all levels, and the value of an academic degree depends heavily on the name of the institution offering it. Thus higher education reinforces inequality, not reduces it.

This discussion prompts a final reflection on the role of education, which economists are prone, perhaps wrongly, to treat as an investment good. Suppose instead one treats it as a form of consumption, done for its own sake? In that case, *public education* at all levels *does* reduce inequality. It does so by providing *to the parents*, at low or zero price, a consumption good that many value but could not otherwise afford. It is therefore exactly equivalent to an increase in household money income, and highly progressive, in that the proportional effect is much greater for those with less to begin with.

Can Progressive Income Taxes Reduce Inequalities?

A more direct way to level out living standards is to impose taxes on income, in ways that fall more heavily on those with more income. Progressive income taxes do this by increasing the rate of tax that applies at higher incomes. Taxes on dividends and capital gains have a similar effect—even if the rate is quite low—since these types of income are earned only by those with capital assets, and hence have zero incidence on the poor. Taxes on sales and the Value-Added-Tax fall more heavily on those who consume a larger share of their income, and therefore have the opposite effect, but it is unrecorded, as we shall discuss later.

In the Second World War and for the quarter-century that followed, top progressive income tax rates remained very high, having peaked at 92 percent on the highest incomes. The purpose of such high rates, under wartime conditions, was not to collect the tax. It was to dissuade companies from paying any salaries that would exceed the lower bound of the bracket to which the highest rate applied. The underlying purpose was to prevent wartime profiteering, which would have been very bad for civilian and military morale. And since almost all high incomes in wartime were a matter of payments from companies, this policy was very effective. High incomes were kept largely under control during the war, while price controls and wage increases at the bottom, as well as massively increased women's employment, meant unprecedented equalization of household incomes and household consumption.

In peacetime, inevitably, problems arose. Lobbies found ways to get Congress to allow reductions in reported income for particular purposes, such as oil or timber "depletion." Companies, flush with profits, found ways to spend them on agreeable living for their top leadership, who could enjoy downtown skyscrapers, penthouse apartments, executive washrooms, corporate aircraft, and retreats, free of tax. And certain individuals also emerged for whom the high income tax rates would bite, because they lacked the umbrella of a corporate shell. This was true for top actors, actresses, and other performers, top lawyers and other professionals, some writers and artists, and for big-league athletes, all of whom were likely to feel that their incomes were due to exceptional personal merit, effort, and appeal, and should therefore not be limited by measures designed to prevent profiteering. It was probably not accidental that the three key figures behind the Tax Reform Act of 1986, which lowered top rates dramatically and definitively, were Representative Jack Kemp and Senator Bill Bradley, former professional athletes, and President Ronald Reagan, a former movie star.

Nevertheless, the income tax remains progressive, and the effect of taxes alone on the equality of the distribution of disposable income can be measured directly for many countries, by comparing Gini coefficients of gross and net income. For advanced social democracies, the effect is on the order of 10 to 15 percent. It is a bit less for the United States, but still substantial. For most developing and transition economies, on the other hand, the effect is approximately zero, as tax measures do not significantly diminish the advantages that the rich hold over the middle classes and the poor.

Does Social Insurance Reduce Inequalities?

The United States has a large number of social insurance programs, of which the major ones are Social Security, Medicare, and Medicaid; others include unemployment insurance, nutrition assistance, and deposit insurance, as well as the Earned Income Tax Credit, which acts as a form of "real wage insurance" for working people who have uneven access to work, and therefore varying income, over the course of a taxable year. Of these, Social Security is the largest, and although it is principally an old-age pension program, it also encompasses disability insurance and survivors' benefits; about a third of Social Security benefits are paid to survivors and especially to children of beneficiaries.

It seems intuitive that social insurance reduces inequalities. After all, the Social Security system imposes a tax—the payroll tax—on working people who do not have parents of their own to support, while paying a benefit—the monthly check—to some people who do not have children otherwise willing or able to support them. Both of these effects are pro-fairness; in the first case, because working people without parents have less of a burden than working people with them; in the second, because the elderly whose children would otherwise support them are better off than the elderly without this source of support. In both cases, the effect of the system is to take a burden that was previously imposed on the family, an arbitrary and unreliable unit, and shift it to the society as a whole, with the benefit criterion depending in part on need and in part on past work and earnings.

Still, one must be careful about how precise effects are likely to appear in the data, for two reasons. First, the funding mechanism for Social Security consists of a tax on payrolls, which is capped at a certain level, currently $117,000 per year. Those who earn more than the cap do not pay Social Security tax on their income above the cap, and hence their effective tax rate is less. Those who have non-wage earnings, for instance from capital assets, pay no Social Security tax on those earnings. So the payroll tax is regressive, and has the effect of increasing the inequality of disposable income compared to what it would be if the payroll tax did not exist, but Social Security benefits were still paid.

What about the benefits side? Here a little reflection is in order. Suppose a modest public pension flows to a family that already has a modest working income, in support of an elderly parent? In most cases, but depending on the original household income level, the effect will be to raise that household's total disposable income *toward* the mean, and therefore to reduce overall income inequality. But now suppose that instead of contributing to his children's household income, the elderly parent hops on a motorcycle, or into an RV, and drives off to a sunny new trailer home in the west of Florida or the south of Texas? In that case, there are now two households instead of one. The first household, with one fewer mouth to feed and one fewer body to care for, is a bit better off than it was before Social Security. The second household, however, has a very low income and is, in fact, borderline poor. Overall household income inequality has now *increased*—even though every individual involved is better off—having chosen freely to live independently—than they were before.

In the data, as we have seen earlier, there is a concept called *market inequality*, which represents the inequality of incomes across households from market sources, namely wages and earnings from capital assets. In all advanced countries, this measure is very unequal, and the shift from the "market" to the "gross" concept of income inequality involves a large reduction in the Gini coefficient. But as we have just seen, even if the effect of social insurance on measured inequality is to reduce it, that effect may be small compared to the raising effect of social insurance on market inequalities. For since public pensions are non-market, they create households that would not otherwise exist, and that in many cases have *zero* market income. This is not a bad thing—but it is a cautionary tale about the numbers.

The presence of large numbers of independent non-working elderly households has another interesting effect on the data: a large share of households within the lowest income decile—the bottom 10 percent—have market incomes that come exclusively from capital assets. These households are, very likely, not poor at all. They are merely retired, with paid-off mortgages and modest cash flows, met by a large enough reserve of past savings, plus the non-market benefits of Social Security and Medicare. An increase in overall household market income inequality owing to the emergence of a large number of prosperous retirees is a possibility that would have to be watched and discounted in evaluating such a change in the data.

The effect of health insurance on measured income inequality is another imponderable. Once again, there is the tax. Although in the case of Medicare recent changes in law removed the cap, the tax is still regressive since it does not touch non-wage or salary income. And what about the benefits? Do they flow only to those who get sick, and whose bills are paid by the government? Or should they be counted as part of everyone's income, since protection against medical bankruptcy is a good shared by the healthy and the sick alike? Or do the benefits go to the medical providers—to the surgeons and doctors and nurses—to whom they are actually paid and whose non-poor lifestyles they support? These are metaphysical questions, without empirical answers—which does not mean that they are bad questions, only that we are pushing the limits of sensible interpretation of inequality numbers.

Can Reducing Sales Taxes Reduce Inequalities?

For a final issue, let's consider the effect of sales and Value-Added-Taxes on household income inequality. These taxes are undoubtedly regressive, since they fall on consumption but not on savings, and since saving is the prerogative of those whose incomes exceed what they need to spend. But how does this regressive effect show up in inequality measures?

The answer is: it does not. Sales taxes have no effect on market income or the inequality thereof. They have no effect on transfer payments and pensions, and therefore none on the inequality of household gross income. And they have no effect on "post-tax" disposable income, since disposable income is counted by subtracting direct taxes from gross income. Disposable income, in short, is what you take to the store, but the sales tax is determined by what you choose to purchase. It acts as a drain on final consumption—and the inequality of final consumption is not part of the data picture that we have.

So it appears that in spite of all our care and efforts, we are still missing an important element in the effect of government policy on the distribution of final household welfare—and a nasty element at that, much more harmful to the poor than to the rich.

Yet on the other hand, are consumption standards really driven so far apart by regressive sales taxation? That, too, is not entirely clear, in a society like the United States (though much less so in Europe) where retailing is rough-and-tumble and where inexpensive imports are available at low tariffs and prices. It may be that a significant effect of trade policy, income inequality, and sales taxation—taken together—as practiced in the United States is to foster the creation of discount outlets, where merchandise available to (but not wanted by) wealthier people in boutiques and department stores eventually comes to be sold to those of modest means, who are therefore able to extend their consumption dollars per unit of tax paid. (The same is true, for example, of the market for used cars, furniture, and for many other items.) To that extent, physical consumption differences are not so great as they would be otherwise, and the consequence of income inequalities lies principally in the amenities associated with the experience of shopping and the other burdens of daily life.

Conclusion

Is the reduction of measured household income inequality a policy goal in and of itself? The answer is, perhaps, yes: it appears that an economy with a lower degree of wage and salary inequality generally works better and is also viewed by its inhabitants as more fair. A higher minimum wage, a greater degree of union coverage, and the Earned Income Tax Credit appear to have very little downside. Progressive taxes can discourage excessive before-tax incomes, and help to moderate their effects when they occur. Social insurance protects the weak and the vulnerable, and in that sense it definitely reduces inequalities in the country at large.

But so far as the specific effect of progressive policies on measures of household income inequality, the answer has to be qualified. For the case of the United States, we have seen enough reasons that the measure of household income inequality may *not* correspond with the movement toward a more fair, prosperous, and just society, particularly if, in a fair society, we value the right of people to live independently on modest incomes. It is important to bear in mind that some of the most vital egalitarian programs, such as Social Security, may or may not reduce the Gini coefficient. That fact—if it is a fact—does not make them any less vital.

There are many remaining puzzles and challenges in this area. Go forth and study—but be careful!

11

A NOTE ON WEALTH
AND POWER

"Wealth, as Mr. Hobbes says, is power." Adam Smith wrote that, and I've already quoted it. It is the beginning and end of economic comments on the subject of wealth. And power.

We have only touched lightly on wealth so far in this volume, and for a reason: though a vast and important topic, the definition of wealth is uncertain, the measure of wealth is difficult, the data are sparse and the conclusions depend heavily on particular choices of research technique. For all the limitations of studies of pay and income, there is simply much more information available, and it is therefore possible to make much more headway, in the study of those issues.

What Is Wealth?

As noted in Chapter 1, wealth is commonly defined as *financial wealth*, namely cash on hand and the money value of marketable assets. But wealth also includes the value of tangible and illiquid assets that cannot be so readily sold, including land, houses, Old Masters, jewels, signed letters from Presidents, and antique musical instruments. And it includes the value of income streams and insurance rights that cannot be transacted or (for the most part) encumbered, including Social Security, Medicare, Medicaid, and similar public programs. For some economists, the prospective value of inalienable credentials (such as your college diploma) and of offices (such as a tenured chair at a university) should also be included. However, no known data set goes so far as to estimate such things. And against these assets, one must subtract the value of debts; net wealth or net equity is the difference between these two valuations.

A basic fact about net financial wealth is that the vast majority of the world's population has none. Indeed, much of the US population has no net financial wealth, and this is especially true for African American and immigrant households. Even for the middle class, the value of financial assets may be smaller than the value of a mortgage debt, held against housing. Even a relatively prosperous middle-class family, with a steady job or two, an owned home, and no great worries, can show little or no (or even negative) net financial wealth. (In fact, it's a very common condition, sometimes known as being "house-poor.") Net financial wealth is the privilege, very largely, of the wealthy. Meanwhile, debt is the mark of those who are *not* in the top echelons, as Figure 11.1 shows.

How Is Wealth Distributed in America?

Wealth is therefore much more concentrated than income; it always has been and always will be. However, the degree of that concentration depends greatly on what is included in the definition. Financial wealth is the most unequal. Housing wealth is far more equally held, with about 60 percent of US households owning their homes, and—under what were once considered normal conditions—enjoying some net equity, or housing wealth, in those homes.

Social Security, Medicare, and Medicaid wealth are the major forms held by most of the elderly, and the right to Medicaid and other forms of public assistance may be the only form of "wealth" accessible to the poor. Are such things really

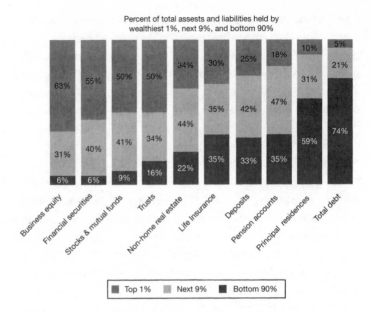

Percent of total assests and liabilities held by
wealthiest 1%, next 9%, and bottom 90%

Figure 11.1 Shares of assets and liabilities held by deciles, the United States.
Source: Edward Wolff, New York University.

wealth? One may think not—but the proper comparison is not
to the condition of the rich, but to the conditions that would
face lower-income households if they did not have access to
these programs. Clearly, they would be much worse off; that
which protects them is wealth.

Social Security and other insurance programs are often
criticized for imposing financial liabilities on the government,
and hence on the nation. By extending the calculations out to
seventy-five years and longer, and by taking a low rate of discount, one can make the number of this "contingent liability"
almost as large as you like, and it is frequently counted in the
tens of trillions of dollars. However, the accounting principle
of double-entry bookkeeping tells us that if there is a contingent liability, then somewhere there must be a corresponding
asset. In this case, that asset is the "contingent wealth" of the
US working population, who—if they are lucky and live long

enough—will enjoy the Social Security benefits and medical protections in the same years ahead. Since the working population that "owes" Social Security today is the same one that will draw benefits later on, it is hard to see why they should complain about a "national" liability that is, to them, a form of wealth.

How Do We Measure Financial Wealth?

Measurement and distribution of financial wealth are the easiest to study; one simply needs to take the market valuation of financial portfolios and compare them. That is how we "know" that Bill Gates, for instance, is (or perhaps, was) the "world's richest person." We know Gates's wealth because we know his holdings of stock, mainly in Microsoft, and we know the market price of that stock at any given time. Gates's portfolio is calculated by multiplying one number against the other.

But is Mr. Gates really "the world's richest man"? Is there no oil sheikh, whose assets include control of the world's greatest resource pools, richer than he? Are there no old magnates, with vast half-hidden land-holdings, or ships on the high seas, whose total value they would prefer not be known? No Russian oligarchs worth more than he? We cannot be sure of that; given the scale of looting in post-Soviet Russia, there could be quite a number of those with more spending money than Bill Gates. It does seem likely that Mr. Gates's standing came about, in part, because US laws require a degree of disclosure not present in other countries, and perhaps also in part because the marketing of Microsoft was thought to benefit from the perceived success of its CEO. It seems quite rare, in the American technology world, that the leaders of the main corporations object to the publicity surrounding their wealth. In Germany, by contrast, where many companies are privately held, great gains in wealth occur largely as unrealized capital gains; they are unrecorded, undisclosed, and untaxed.

Then again, is all Mr. Gates's wealth really "there"? Consider his situation before the creation of the Bill and Melinda Gates Foundation. His wealth was heavily concentrated in his large ownership share in Microsoft stock. Could he have sold that stock at the market price? Of course not. Stock prices are quoted at the margin. A small amount can be transacted at the going price; if more is offered, the price falls. If when Gates was worth $50 billion he had tried to turn, say, 40 percent of his holdings into cash, he would have realized far less than $20 billion, and the remainder of his holdings would have turned to dust. One reason that people in the position of Bill and Melinda Gates eventually transfer their holdings to a foundation is the risk of an unplanned-for taxable event, such as the estate tax, which would force liquidation of private holdings with catastrophic effects on their price.

The practice of paying high corporate officers in stock of their own companies creates an interesting anomaly in the distribution of pay within the corporation. Typical practice in countries where top management earn salaries (such as Japan) is for a differential between the average pay and the CEO pay on the order of thirty or forty to one. This is a healthy difference, but minor compared with the 411-to-1 differential that prevailed among the top 500 corporations in the United States in the year 2000. That difference, in turn, was driven by a handful of companies, in the technology sector, who were experiencing massively high valuations in the gold rush of that moment. After the Great Financial Crisis the ratio fell to 181.5 to 1 in 2009.

Comparisons of CEO to worker pay are a staple of popular articles on income inequality, but it's worth bearing in mind two facts. First, there are only 500 people in CEO positions of the top 500 corporations at any one time, and the average compensation figures are strongly skewed by the handful at the very top of the pile. So the issue affects only a handful of households, out of well over a hundred million, at any given time. Second, CEOs are not the most highly paid people in the economy. There are quite a few hedge fund managers, for instance, and private-equity tycoons, against whose incomes those of mere management, even in the biggest banks and corporations, seem ordinary.

But things that the very wealthy would prefer to conceal often do stay concealed.

How Does Wealth Translate to Power?

Let us count the ways.

In the United States, there are campaign contributions—really just the beginning of this story.

There is the ability to lobby Congress, the White House, and the regulatory agencies.

There is the ability to provide employment to out-of-work officeholders, and to place one's own staff in high positions in the government ("Government Sachs").

There is the ability to control the nominating processes of both major political parties, so that all electoral choices are made from among candidates acceptable to the donor class.

There is control of the mass media and influence over the educational system.

There is the ability to suppress the votes of inconvenient populations.

Wealth is indeed power—as Mr. Hobbes said.

What about a Financial Wealth Tax?

In *Capital in the 21st Century*, Thomas Piketty made a splash by proposing an annual progressive tax on financial assets, as a way of reducing inequalities in the world economy. His idea was that there would be a yearly assessment of the market valuation of financial wealth, and a small percentage levy that would (presumably) go to each country in proportion to the wealth located there. The tax would, of course, have to be implemented evenly on a worldwide basis; otherwise, wealth would merely flow from jurisdictions that had the tax to those that did not.

What would be the consequences of enacting such a tax, assuming that it could be done on the requisite worldwide basis? To begin with, consider the problem of valuation: What is the financial value of a particular portfolio when considered on an annual basis? Is it the value on a given date? In that case, one might expect values to fall before the tax date, as people shift from taxable to non-taxable assets, and to rise thereafter. Is it the average value over the year? In that case, day-by-day and even minute-by-minute record-keeping might be required.

Further, suppose the tax were enacted and portfolios could be valued on an ongoing basis. In that case, to pay the tax, non-money financial assets, such as stocks and bonds, would be subject to a levy based on their market value. Bill Gates, when he was worth $100 billion, might have to come up with $1.5 billion in hard cash per year, for instance. Where would he get it? Perhaps by selling Microsoft stock. The effect would be surely to reduce the market value of Microsoft, and therefore of Gates, and therefore his tax liability! By how much? It's difficult to say; that would depend on the effect of such selling on the open market for the stock—on whether there was a buyer on hand. But if Gates held (say) 70 percent of Microsoft, then 1.5 percent of that would translate into over 3 percent of the remaining holdings. Enough to tank the stock? Depends . . .

This bit of thought forces a question: What public policy goal is served by forcing the partial liquidation of productive assets, and by forcing down their price? None that one can think of, quite apart from the effect on the distribution of financial wealth.

In any case, as Piketty admits, this proposal is "utopian." And if the proposal is utopian, which is a synonym for futile, then why make it? Thought experiments are all very well, but one should not spend too much time on them at the expense of practical proposals.

What about a Land Tax?

A much older and yet, to this day, still more promising alternative to taxing financial wealth is to tax land value, including the value of mineral and energy resources in the ground. The economic concept behind this idea is that of Ricardian rent—the argument that rents (which are inherently unproductive) flow to the owners of the fixed and non-reproducible asset, namely land. By taxing land and minerals, one reaches the least defensible forms of accumulated wealth, while at the same time doing the least to distort market decisions as between capital investment and hiring of labor. And there is another advantage: unlike financial wealth, land stays put. It exists in fixed jurisdictions with registered ownership; all the taxing authorities need to do is to send an appraiser, and then a bill. Local property taxes already work this way; however, in the United States landowner opposition to land taxes has been fierce, and many states are barred by their constitutions from levying property tax on a statewide basis. In California, notoriously, even local property taxes were capped in the late 1970s by a ballot measure strongly supported by wealthy landholding interests.

Land taxation has been for a century the program of the followers of the nineteenth-century American economist Henry George, whose influence was vast around the world a century ago. One of his followers was the Chinese revolutionary Sun Yat-Sen, founder of the Republic of China in 1911. And Maoist China, by conducting an early war against landlords, ended up having the world economy most like the Georgist program in the modern age. But instead of taxing land value, the Chinese state actually owns it, and collects the land rent for itself. By doing this, Chinese municipalities and provinces have enjoyed ample revenue from which to make capital improvements, which is why Chinese cities have been able to grow like weeds in the reform era, without turning into slums, as is the fate of so much urbanization in the developing world. And as improvements are made, values rise, and so do rents! China is therefore also able to get away with little to no taxation of sales or wages or incomes; the land rent provides a very substantial share of what the government needs.

How Do Estate and Gift Taxes Reduce Inequalities?

One American tax has played an important role in controlling the growth of private fortunes in the past century. This is the estate and gift tax, introduced by Theodore Roosevelt in the trust-busting era. The estate and gift tax imposes a high rate of tax—in recent years as high as 55 percent, though lower today, on estates valued at above a certain threshold. The tax is assessed just once, on the death of the estate owner, and it is paid by the estate before the remainder can be distributed to the heirs.

The principle behind the estate tax is that accumulations should be allowed for the first generation, as a reward for the talent or luck that made them possible, but that dynasties should be avoided and that later generations should not enjoy unlimited access to the founders' wealth.

And there is a further idea, which is that the tax can be avoided altogether if the fortune is donated to an authorized nonprofit institution, such as a hospital, church, museum, library, or university, or placed in a philanthropic foundation before the death of the holder. This institutional arrangement, which appears to exist nowhere else, has had a profound effect on civic and cultural life in the United States, transferring vast resources over the years into buildings, scholarships, and healthcare facilities. It is in substantial measure responsible for the quality of American universities, including public universities, which unlike their counterparts in socialist and social-democratic countries, do not have to rely on often-strapped and stingy legislatures for their sole support. Meanwhile the simple recycling of accumulated fortunes into construction and employment generates about 8 percent of American employment, and is partly responsible for the relatively low rates of unemployment characteristic of the modern United States, when compared to Europe.

Estate and gift taxes take the long view about wealth accumulations, on the theory that the drive to accumulate cannot be and should not be suppressed—but at the same time, the accumulations themselves become damaging when they fall under the control of the privileged, feckless, and lazy brats that the original founders of great fortunes tend to spawn. There is vast and irrefutable evidence that the judgment of President Theodore Roosevelt on this matter was entirely correct.

A FINAL DIGRESSION

DOES ECONOMIC EQUALITY LEAD TO VICTORY IN WAR?

Not every economic or political attribute is restricted to economic implications alone. And not every aspect of inequality is something everyone needs to know. Therefore we now abandon the question-and-answer format that we have used so far. In this epilogue we take up a side question, but one that may capture the reader's imagination, as it captured this author's while he and several talented students were doing the work.

The question is whether egalitarian societies do better on the battlefield than their unequal opponents. It is prompted in part by a general sense that comradeship is a military virtue, in part by casual observation that wartime mobilizations tend to have radically equalizing properties, and in part by the rise and fall of a parallel thesis—the "democratic victory" hypothesis, in the political science literature.

In a pioneering book for a decade of violence, Dan Reiter and Allan Stam (2002) argue that political democracies have a "fourth virtue": victory in war. They attribute this primarily to better choices of when to initiate wars, to better military leadership, and to better morale and stronger commitment among the fighting forces. The interest of the hypothesis, at a moment when the (ostensibly democratic) United States had attacked Afghanistan and was about to launch an invasion of Saddam Hussein's Iraq, was evident at the time.

The idea that military decision might rest heavily on a single variable is seductive. Yet even allowing an elastic definition of what democracy is, there haven't been that many wars pitting democratic against non-democratic countries. Reiter and Stam's entire case rests on just 34 examples of democracies at war from 1816 to 1990, of which only 15 represent cases where the democracy is classed as the initiator. Of the 34 conflicts, democracies prevailed in 26, or 74 percent. It is only when Reiter and Stam distinguish between initiators and targets in warfare that the percentage of democratic victories rises to 93 percent, or 14 cases out of 15. It's not much.

But if the presence of democracy has some power to explain military outcomes, perhaps another variable will have even more?

How about Equality?

From a research standpoint, the hypothesis of *egalitarian victory* has several significant advantages over the democratic hypothesis. Most notably, it can be applied in principle to all wars between well-defined pairs of major combatants. One party is always more equal, and the other less so. In the case of regional or global wars, the comparison may be applied (with less assurance) to well-defined pair-wise military fronts. The limitation is not conceptual, but only a matter of measurement.

The egalitarian victory hypothesis also avoids a thorny problem facing the *democratic victory* alternative, namely that of distinguishing between "initiators" and "targets," a distinction deemed necessary to excuse cases when democracies lost wars that they would probably have avoided if they could have. Egalitarian victory refers to conditions *at the moment of military decision,* by which time the attribution of blame for the start of the war has often lost relevance. Framed this way, the hypothesis also allows the possibility that economic conditions can evolve during the course of war.

Why might the more equal belligerent enjoy a military advantage? For three reasons, in principle: First, egalitarian countries have stronger social solidarity, and therefore better military morale.[1] Second, unequal countries often structure their armed forces to handle internal regime security, at the expense of efficiency in meeting external threats.[2] Third, highly unequal countries face a problem of loyalty in the lower ranks. An egalitarian adversary will often be seen as a liberator by at least some substantial part of the population, and if prudent the party with that advantage will use it.

There are three types of evidence that help test this idea. First, there are cases where comparative economic inequality can be measured directly. Second, there are cases where reasonable inferences about comparative economic inequality may be drawn by analogy to measurements or from other political and economic evidence. Third, there are cases where inferences may be drawn from literary or historical sources.

Taking these together, the evidence for the egalitarian victory hypothesis is remarkably strong. It also seems that the pursuit of the free market economic policy agenda[3]—which tends to increase inequality—may work to undermine the effectiveness of the military forces required to underpin and, in some cases, to implement that agenda. Conversely, even relatively poor populations that band together to resist the encroachment of free markets, global corporations, and the mercenaries who advance their causes may enjoy a military advantage, hitherto unnoticed.

The hypothesis is that when two countries fight a war, the more economically equal usually prevails. There is

1. This was thought true of the US and Soviet armies in the Second World War, though somewhat less so of the British.
2. Ngo Dinh Diem's Army of the Republic of Vietnam was a notorious example, but they could be multiplied.
3. Known outside the United States as "neoliberal" economic policy, or the "Washington Consensus."

a need therefore to define three terms: *country*, *war*, and *economically equal*.

To begin with, let us examine wars between territorial nation-states in the recognizably modern sense of that term. Greek city-states qualify, as do the Golden Hordes of Tamurlane, the Aztecs of Mexico, and the Incas of Peru. Tribes such as the Cherokee or the Zulu or the Mahdi Army do not, notwithstanding egalitarian social structures and considerable fighting prowess in many cases. It is accurate to describe these entities as "nations," but it seems a stretch to qualify them as countries. Civil wars only qualify if carried out between territorial entities claiming country status: the US Civil War qualifies, but the Spanish Civil War would not.[4]

War is defined as a conflict between organized military forces. Coups and national wars of liberation are excluded, except where they were part of a defined bi-national or multi-national conflict, as was true in the case of Vietnam. Massacres, riots, and revolutions are also not wars. For a list of candidate wars, we use the well-established Correlates of War data set for conflicts going back to 1815.

Finally, there is the problem of defining *economic equality*. Here the emphasis is on relative equality in the structure of economic earnings, especially pay, as this represents our best measure of the social structure of a country. It is a variable for which the most direct and reliable transnational measurements in the modern period exist, and so the best chance of making reasonable inferences with respect to earlier times.

Equality and Victory, 1963–1999

The first body of evidence consists of 32 international conflicts between recognized states from 1962 to the

---

4. The Chinese and Russian civil wars were fought between entities that held well-defined territories for long times; however, despite the obvious temptation to count them for our hypothesis, we exclude them.

present. For each conflict, the UTIP-UNIDO measure of pay inequality for the year the conflict ended, or the year the state exited the conflict, is appropriate. Of 32 conflicts and 42 potential pairwise comparisons (in the cases of multiparty wars), actual data are available for 23 conflicts and 31 match-ups.[5]

In short, for the most part, in 42 pair-wise comparisons, the more egalitarian country seems to have won 29 times, there are five undecidable cases, and just eight exceptions. Of the exceptions, three relate to India and Pakistan, two relate to Cyprus, and one pairing (Saudi Arabia–Iraq in 1991) pits a country that was a minor player in a war plainly decided by the armed forces of the United States. If the data are correct, the India-Pakistan cases discriminate in favor of the democratic victory hypothesis against the egalitarian victory hypothesis, but they are the only clear-cut examples so far seen, and in any event Pakistan's defeat was decisive only in 1971. At that time, Pakistan included modern Bangladesh, a much poorer region than West Pakistan, and although measures do not exist it is possible (perhaps likely) that the combined country was more unequal than India.

A substantial share of the measurable conflicts represents pairings in the Middle East, with Israel on one side and various Arab states on the other. In the early days, Israel had a strong collective tradition, and it prevailed several times against larger monarchies, oligarchies, and dictatorships. More recently, the adversary Israel faces has become ascetic and egalitarian in ways that emulate the past of Zionism, while Israel has experienced one of the largest proportionate increases in inequality we observed. Meanwhile, Israel's

5. Where data are only available for years other than the year the conflict ceased, we imputed data for the ending year from the nearest available measurement. Of the 31 comparisons, 13 use imputed data; the median interval from which data are imputed is 2 years. The Mauritanian-Senegalese Border War is excluded due to an 11-year gap in data.

comparative military effectiveness has clearly declined: it was chased from South Lebanon by Hezbollah, and it has failed to defeat Palestinian resistance in Gaza, the effective leadership of which has passed from the autocratic Al-Fatah movement to the ascetic Hamas.

The value of this approach is demonstrated by the fact that in 13 of the 31 comparisons the democratic victory thesis is unable to make a prediction because neither of the states involved was democratic. Of these 13 cases, the equality thesis correctly predicted 11.[6]

Since wars always involve a more equal and a less equal contestant, the egalitarian victory hypothesis disregards the distinction between initiator and target, which is in any event too open to manipulation to be entirely trustworthy.

In sum, an analysis of the best available modern data for equality shows that it is a strong predictor of success in inter-state warfare. This analysis also shows that equality applies successfully to a larger universe of cases than the democratic victory thesis, and its predictive power is at least equally good, if one disregards the initiator/target filter.

Equality and Victory: 1783–1962

The canonical debut of the modern nation-state comes with the creation of the American and the French Republics, both of which were immediately cast into wars against imperial opponents using, in part, mercenary forces. The republic founded on the idea that "all men are created equal" fought its way to victory in 1783, while that founded on *liberté, egalité, fraternité* achieved surprising victory over multiple enemies in 1799. The fledgling United States then suffered ignominious defeat in even-more-egalitarian Canada in 1812, before redeeming itself in battle at New Orleans against the British on January 8, 1815,

---

6. The incorrectly predicted cases were Saudi Arabia against Iraq in the First Gulf War and Ethiopia against Eritrea.

in a battle in which Creoles and free men of color were deeply engaged.

Meanwhile, France had regressed from Republic to Empire, and as Napoleon became more imperial he became less militarily effective; as early as 1803 he was beaten in Haiti by the freed slaves led by Toussaint L'Ouverture. It is impossible from the present remove to judge the relative equalities of (say) France and Russia as a whole in 1812, but it is very plausible to argue that the French Empire, whose Grande Armée was drawn heavily from Poland and other Slavic lands, was less egalitarian than the Russians it faced at Borodino.

The American Civil War was, from the point of view of both sides, a conflict between territorial entities with well-defined borders. The Confederacy considered itself to be, and in 1860 for practical purposes was, an independent nation-state. It was also a slave-owners oligarchy, commanding the loyalty neither of its black slaves—many of whom became Union soldiers—nor of many of its property-less white settlers, especially in such regions as Western Virginia (which seceded from Virginia in order to stay in the Union), and eastern Tennessee (from which Lincoln's 1864 running mate, Andrew Johnson, was chosen). The Union, on the other hand, was a land of relatively small farmers and an emerging industrial working class; by 1864 it was arguably (after Haiti) the most egalitarian republic in history. Karl Marx saw the social difference clearly, and penned his famous letter of congratulation to Abraham Lincoln on his re-election, which begins, "From the commencement of the titanic strife, the workingmen of Europe felt instinctively that the star-spangled banner carried the destiny of their class." Enough said on that score.

In the 1850s, the rising bourgeois states of France and Britain defeated the decaying Russian Empire in the Crimea. In 1870, France was beaten by Prussia in a lightning campaign that ended at Sedan. Prussia was at that time an emerging industrial power, but by 1870 France had been a retrograde empire under Napoleon II for two decades.

By 1914, on the other hand, France had been a republic for 44 years, and its industrial development had progressed to a point comparable to Germany's, though in a smaller country. A strong socialist workers' movement had by then emerged; arguably France in 1914 was at least as egalitarian as the German Empire. The comparison with the United Kingdom is less clear, but in any event the result on the Western Front was stalemate to the point of exhaustion, resolved only by the intervention in 1917 of that still relatively egalitarian republic, the United States.

On other First World War fronts, Germany was surely more egalitarian than Tsarist Russia, which collapsed early in the war. The decrepit Ottoman Empire was a major casualty of the war, but on the other hand the secular, nationalist, and relatively egalitarian Turkey that emerged from its ruins proved effective against the British at Gallipoli, and in driving the Greeks from Asia Minor right after the war.

In 1932–1935 Bolivia defeated Paraguay in a nasty conflict known as the Chaco Wars. According to the UTIP-UNIDO data, Paraguay is the most unequal country of Latin America and one of the most unequal in the world; Bolivia (alongside fellow-combatants Argentina and Brazil) is unequal but less so. Admittedly, that one was three against one, so the outcome may be overdetermined.

The Second World War presents a plethora of comparisons. Of these, perhaps the most important are the Soviet Union against Germany, the United States against Japan, the United States against Germany and Italy, and Great Britain against Germany. In all of these, we believe, the plausible case is that the more egalitarian country prevailed. As Galbraith and Ferguson (2001) have shown, war mobilization in the United States produced a radical leveling of the wage and income structure within a year after the start of the war. Something similar undoubtedly happened in Britain, though not in

Germany, where social structures were rigorously preserved by the Nazis and women were excluded, largely, from the industrial workforce.

The Korean War of 1950–1953 provides a very interesting case, insofar as both halves of the peninsula were cut from the same cloth at that time, while the newly established People's Republic of China and the United States were then both among the world's most egalitarian countries. The result of the war— not surprisingly from the standpoint of our hypothesis—was a draw.

In the wars of the 1950s, nationalists in Vietnam and Algeria chased the French from their colonies. France was a moderately egalitarian democratic republic in those days, but the Vietnamese and Algerians, though not democratic, were surely more egalitarian. Similarly, the (democratic) Dutch were forced to exit (undemocratic) Indonesia, where a strong communist presence continued until it was savagely extinguished in 1965. In 1961, in a small engagement, a lightly armed Cuban militia defeated a CIA-backed brigade of exiles at the Bay of Pigs.

In all of these cases, it appears, the more egalitarian side prevailed, notwithstanding a much weaker industrial system and lower per capita income. In each of the cases just mentioned, egalitarian victory occurred, despite the fact that in most of these cases the losing party would qualify as a democracy while the winning side would not.

What is striking about all this, in short, is not how easy it is to make a plausible argument for the thesis that the more egalitarian power usually prevails in conflict, notwithstanding adverse differences in average income level, industrial development, or democratic status. What is striking is how difficult it is to identify unmistakable opposing cases. Unambiguous cases of the more unequal state prevailing in bi-national conflict undoubtedly exist. But looking at a list of modern wars reveals very few instances where one is tempted to dig deeply to try to find them.

Classical Cases: Athens to Agincourt

The saga of the Peloponnesian Wars provides a cautionary tale, known to all schoolchildren, of the contest of democracy against a hyper-egalitarian martial state. Reiter and Stam quote Herodotus on the rise of Athens, but while they take him to be speaking of popular government, *equality* is the word he actually uses:

> It is not only in respect of one thing but of everything that equality and free speech are clearly a good; take the case of Athens, which under the rule of princes proved to be no better in war than any of her neighbors, but once rid of those princes, was far the first of all. (Reiter and Stam, 61)

Very curiously, the index of *Democracies at War* contains no entry for Sparta.

The Punic Wars are a bit harder to read, as both Rome and Carthage were empires, though the former had been a republic and the reach of the latter was greater, making it possibly less egalitarian on both counts. The decline and fall of the Roman Empire is another school tale; by the time Alaric sacked Rome in AD 410 it was surely far less egalitarian than its attackers. Indeed, Procopius of Caesarea gives an account of just how the inequalities of Rome led to its capture:

> Among the youths in the army whose beards had not yet grown, but who had just come of age, [Alaric] chose out three hundred whom he knew to be of good birth and possessed of valor beyond their years, and told them secretly that he was about to make a present of them to certain of the patricians in Rome, pretending that they were slaves. And he instructed them that, as soon as they got inside the houses of those men, they should display much gentleness

and moderation and serve them eagerly in whatever tasks should be laid upon them by their owners; and he further directed them that not long afterwards, on an appointed day at midday, when all those who were to be their masters would most likely be already asleep after their meal, they should all come to the gate called Salarian and with a sudden rush kill the guards, who would have no previous knowledge of the plot, and open the gates as quickly as possible. (Procopius 1953–1954)

Neither Rome nor Carthage figures in the index to Reiter and Stam.

Like the armies of Alexander, the Golden Hordes of Tamurlane, Genghis Khan and Attila owed their vast military success in part to a comparatively flat hierarchy; nomadic tribes everywhere are more broadly egalitarian than the territorial domains they ravage. The Moghul conquest of India provides an even stronger case, for it was a religious war, in which the Islamic armies from the North repudiated the Hindu caste system that they faced. Islam won its Indian converts heavily from the lowest castes.

The Spanish conquest of the Americas likewise took advantage of divisions in the deeply hierarchical territorial empires that the small bands of Cortes and Pizarro stumbled into. On the other hand, few would doubt that Elizabethan England was more egalitarian than the Spain of Philip II; Sir Francis Drake epitomizes the rise of the common privateer on merit rather than birth.

The final example is perhaps the most clear-cut. At Agincourt, the British triumph rests in the historical record on the military effectiveness of the Welsh longbowmen—a yeomen's cohort with no equivalent in the French army. We also have the Shakespearean version, in the encounter of King Hal, in disguise, with Pistol, on Crispin's Eve:

PISTOL: Discuss unto me; art thou officer?
Or art thou base, common and popular?
KING HENRY V: I am a gentleman of a company.
PISTOL: Trail'st thou the puissant pike?
KING HENRY V: Even so. What are you?
PISTOL: As good a gentleman as the emperor.
KING HENRY V: Then you are a better than the king.

Conclusion

Democracies are, generally speaking, egalitarian in comparison with most other forms of government, and so the hypothesis of democratic victory has a certain amount in common with the hypothesis of egalitarian victory. Where the cases overlap, they explain many of the same things and for similar reasons. However, a focus on equality carries substantially more persuasive power, for at least the following reasons.

First, relatively few wars have had a participant that qualifies as a democracy, and among those that do, the claim of democratic status is often contestable. Democracy is an ideal type. The accepted indicators of democracy are a complex scale of attributes, subject to methodological variation (such as different weightings on different attributes) that might conceivably change the rankings. On the other hand, all wars are in principle between more and less egalitarian combatants. Measurements of inequality done in the manner prescribed are standard and uniform from one country to the next, leaving little room for method-driven variations.

Second, the hypothesis of democratic victory relies heavily on an accurate distinction between initiators and targets. But this is problematic and contestable ground. Initiators can be provoked, as the Austro-Hungarian Empire was in 1914 and the Japanese undoubtedly were in 1941. In any event, the history of how wars started is often written differently by the different contestants. The hypothesis of egalitarian victory focuses on conditions at the moment of military decision, and expresses no interest in how a war may have begun.

Third, where direct measurement is available in the modern period, the egalitarian victory hypothesis accurately predicts the outcome in a wide majority of cases.

Fourth, given what is known about the conditions associated with lower inequality in the modern period, it is possible to make reasonable conjectures about relative inequality for a wide range of earlier wars. While it is always possible that this exercise is contaminated by prior knowledge of the victors, in many cases the differences in social system are so stark as to make the direction of difference, if not its magnitude, reasonably clear-cut. For many earlier wars, literary and historical evidence can be found; indeed the commentary on the importance of solidarity in military effectiveness and the rot that sets in with wealth and hierarchy is virtually omnipresent in classical discussions of military outcomes. In virtually all of these cases, lore and legend hold that the more egalitarian society is likely to prevail.

Fifth and finally, there have been a handful of wars in which democracies were pitted against states *more* egalitarian than themselves, providing a discriminating test of the two conjectures. These were the twentieth century's wars over communism: the Allied expedition to Archangel in 1920, the Korean War, the Bay of Pigs, and the Vietnam War. In all of these cases, the communist country prevailed (or, in the case of Korea, fought a much richer and more powerful country to a draw). In fact, there appears to be no case in which a communist country, however small or underdeveloped, suffered ultimate military defeat at the hands of any democratic or authoritarian state. Not even Socialist Serbia was defeated on the battlefield by the United States in the 70-day war over Kosovo in 1999. That war was resolved by Russian diplomatic intervention.

All of this raises questions that ought to be disturbing to those who believe a free-market economic order can be combined with sustained military dominance in the world today. The Iraq war notably featured an occupying power that has seen inequality rise dramatically since the days of its greatest martial glory a half-century ago. On the other side, the Iraq of 2003 was a highly unequal country of Sunni over-lords and rebellious Shiite underlings. The Iraqi insurgency of 2006—and later the rise of the Islamic State (IS)—represented an egalitarian mini-state in central Iraq, directed by a very effective armed force. IS was eventually held off, and so far continues to be, by an even more egalitarian and secular mili-tary force in Iraqi and also Syrian Kurdistan. From the stand-point of the egalitarian victory hypothesis, it is no surprise that the tables turned.

This digression was adapted from James K. Galbraith, Corwin Priest, and George Purcell, 2007, "Economic Equality and Victory in War: An Empirical Investigation," *Defense and Peace Economics* 18(5): 431–449.

APPENDIX

Measuring Pay Inequality and Estimating Income Inequality: A Technical Note

As described in the text, the Estimated Household Income Inequality data set is derived from Theil measures of pay inequality across industrial sectors, based on payroll and employment measures in the Industrial Statistics of the United Nations Industrial Development Organization. The pay inequality data set is called UTIP-UNIDO. The calculation of EHII from UTIP-UNIDO is based on the following model proposed by Galbraith and Kum (2005):

For each country-year it,

$$\ln(Gini)_{it} = b_0 + b_1 \ln(Theil)_{it} + b_2 \text{ manufacturing share}_{it} + b_3 \text{ income}_{it} + b_4 \text{ household}_{it} + b_5 \text{ gross}_{it} + e_{it}$$

Theil is the UTIP-UNIDO pay inequality measure; *manufacturing share* is the ratio of manufacturing employment to population. The three binary variables control for the types of inequality measures as reported in the source data set, which is the original Deininger-Squire "high-quality" data set. Specifically, the *income* indicator distinguishes between income and expenditure. *Household* differentiates household surveys from per-capita surveys. Lastly, *gross* is a binary indicator that reflects whether the source is gross income or net income. The estimation confirms that each of these binaries has a significant effect on the DS measures.

The estimation of EHII involves two steps. First, the relationship between the DS set of Gini coefficients and UTIP-UNIDO measures of manufacturing pay inequality is established, for 430 exactly overlapping country-year observations in the most recent version. This estimation revealed that when the binaries and manufacturing share are controlled for, there is a very close relationship between the two inequality measures—a sign that both data sets contain reliable information on inequalities.

EHII is then calculated using the estimated coefficients for *Theil* and *manufacturing share*, for a much larger universe of country-year observations. The binary coefficients are set to zero to normalize the estimates on gross household income inequality. The process is explained and the coefficients presented in Galbraith and Kum (2005) and in Galbraith et al. (2014), which presents the most recent updates of both UTIP-UNIDO and EHII.

To construct UTIP-UNIDO, consider a country with n industrial groups, each of which has average pay Y_i and a share in total employment P_i. If Y is the average pay across all sectors in that country, and $\ln()$ is the natural logarithm, then the between-groups component of the Theil index is simply the sum across the n industrial groups of the expression:

$$P_i \left(Y_i / Y \right) * \ln \left(Y_i / Y \right)$$

Because industrial wage data are easily available across many countries, UTIP has been able to construct dense measures of pay inequality distribution across time and space, and to estimate income inequalities in a highly cost-effective manner, filling in gaps in the historical and geographic record with high confidence in the reliability of the estimates.

A Comparison of Inequality Measures for the United States

In Figure A.1 are plotted many of the available measures of income inequality that have been published in recent years for the United States, along with the EHII measure, which is outlined in a thick black line. Measures of market income inequality, gross income inequality, and disposable income inequality are given in varying shades and thicknesses of black and grey, as described in the legend. As one can see, there are a great many diverse measures, with market-income inequalities coming in very high, disposable far lower, and gross income inequality in the middle. However, the three types track each other reasonably well over time, which suggests that the rise in inequality in the United States was due mainly to forces bearing on gross and market income, and not to changes in the redistributive functions of taxes and transfers. Indeed the redistributive function of those programs may have improved, as several measures of disposable income inequality show almost no increase after 1994, even though market and gross income inequalities continued to rise.

The EHII measure tracks one of the measures of gross income inequality very well until 1986. Afterward, they diverge, and EHII fails to pick up the rise in gross income inequalities reported by the CBO in the 1990s and 2000s. As discussed in Chapter 6, the most likely reason is that EHII is based on measures of pay dispersion, and the sawtooth pattern shown in the CBO series coincides exactly with the information-technology boom and then with the real-estate-finance boom and their respective busts. This is strong evidence of the role played by income based on capital-asset prices in the US income distribution. Few other countries exhibit such a strong effect—which may be because it doesn't exist, or if it does, because they fail to measure it effectively in their data. Either way, EHII in most other countries we have examined has a good record of tracking available measures of gross income inequality.

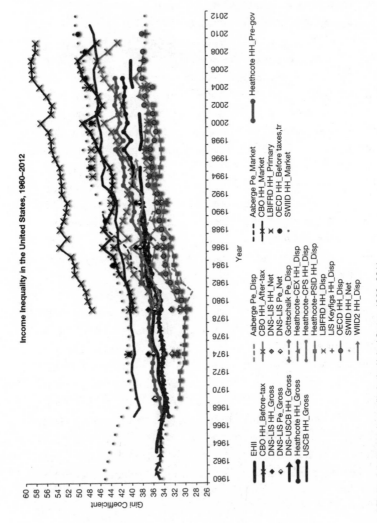

Figure A.1 Income Inequality in the United States, 1960–2011

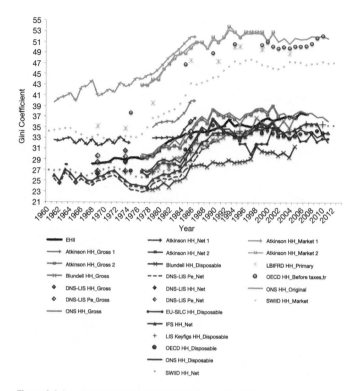

Figure A.2 Income Inequality in the United Kingdom, 1960–2012

An example is the measures for the United Kingdom, presented in Figure A.2. There is a slight capital-asset effect in the 1990s, but by the middle of the first decade of the 2000s it seems to have disappeared.

A list of the source series for the United States is provided here, to give an idea of the vast diversity of concepts and adjustments involved. Readers interested in examining similar comparisons for the United Kingdom and about forty countries in the EHII data set may consult working paper No. 68 on the UTIP site at http://utip.gov.utexas.edu. Béatrice Halbach collected the data and designed these figures.

United States

Aaberge Pe_Disp: *Personal Disposable Income; see note for informa-
    tion on equivalences; based on data from the Panel Study of Income
    Dynamics (PSID), conducted by the Survey Research Centre at
    the University of Michigan; published in Aaberge et al. (2002).*

Aaberge Pe_Market: *Personal Market Income; see note for informa-
    tion on equivalences; based on data from the Panel Study of Income
    Dynamics (PSID), conducted by the Survey Research Centre at
    the University of Michigan; published in Aaberge et al. (2002).*

CBO HH_After-tax: *Household Income after federal taxes and
    after transfers; square root equivalence scale; based on data from
    the Statistics of Income (SOI) collected by the Internal Revenue
    Service (IRS) and from the Annual Social and Economic
    Supplement to the Census Bureau's Current Population Survey
    (CPS), Congressional Budget Office (CBO).*

CBO HH_Before-tax: *Household Income before taxes and after
    transfers; square root equivalence scale; based on data from the
    Statistics of Income (SOI) collected by the Internal Revenue
    Service (IRS) and from the Annual Social and Economic
    Supplement to the Census Bureau's Current Population Survey
    (CPS), Congressional Budget Office (CBO).*

CBO HH_Market: *Household Market Income before taxes
    and before transfers; square root equivalence scale; based
    on data from the Statistics of Income (SOI) collected by the
    Internal Revenue Service (IRS) and from the Annual Social
    and Economic Supplement to the Census Bureau's Current
    Population Survey (CPS), Congressional Budget Office (CBO).*

DNS-LIS HH_Gross: *Household Gross Income, originally obtained
    from LIS Data base, values have a "cs" quality rating according
    to D&S quality rating scale; Deininger and Squire Data set,
    updated version of 1996 data set.*

DNS-LIS Pe_Gross: *Personal Gross Income, originally obtained
    from LIS Data base, values have a "cs" quality rating accord-
    ing to D&S quality rating scale; square root equivalence scale;
    Deininger and Squire Data set, updated version of 1996 data set.*

DNS-LIS HH_Net: *Household Net Income, originally obtained
    from LIS Data base, values have a "cs" quality rating according*

to D&S quality rating scale; Deininger and Squire Data set, updated version of 1996 data set.

DNS-LIS Pe_Net: Personal Gross Income, originally obtained from LIS Data base, values have a "cs" quality rating according to D&S quality rating scale; square root equivalence scale; Deininger and Squire Data set, updated version of 1996 data set.

DNS-USCB HH_Gross: Gross Household Income; no equivalence scale used; originally from the United States Census Bureau (USCB); values have an "accept" quality rating according to D&S quality rating scale; Deininger and Squire Data set, updated version of 1996 data set.

EHII: Estimated Household Income Inequality—University of Texas Inequality Project; gross income, no equivalence scale.

Gottschalk Pe_Disp: Personal Disposable Income; equivalence adjusted for household per capita; based on data from the Current Population Survey (CPS), co-sponsored by the US Census Bureau and the US Bureau of Labor Statistics (BLS); published in Gottschalk and Smeeding (1997).

Heathcote-CEX HH_Disp: Household Disposable Income; OECD equivalence scale; based on data from the Consumer Expenditure Survey (CEX) Interview Surveys, 1980 through 2006, provided by the Bureau of Labor Statistics (BLS); published in Heathcote (2010).

Heathcote-CPS HH_Disp: Household Disposable Income; OECD equivalence scale; based on data from the Current Population Survey (CPS), co-sponsored by the US Census Bureau and the US Bureau of Labor Statistics (BLS); published in Heathcote (2010).

Heathcote HH_Gross: Household Post-government Pre-tax Income; unnamed equivalence scale; based on data from the Current Population Survey (CPS), co-sponsored by the US Census Bureau and the US Bureau of Labor Statistics (BLS); published in Heathcote (2010).

Heathcote HH_Pre-gov: Household Pre-government Income Pre-tax Income; unnamed equivalence scale; based on data from the Current Population Survey (CPS), co-sponsored by the US

Census Bureau and the US Bureau of Labor Statistics (BLS); published in Heathcote (2010).

Heathcote-PSID HH_Disp: Household Disposable Income; OECD equivalence scale; based on data from the Panel Study of Income Dynamics (PSID), conducted by the Survey Research Centre at the University of Michigan; published in Heathcote (2010).

LBIFRD HH_Disp: Household Disposable Income, using the square root equivalence scale; data originally obtained from LIS Database; presented in Caminada and Wang (2011); Leiden Budget Incidence Fiscal Redistribution Database.

LBIFRD HH_Primary: Household Primary Income, using the square root equivalence scale; data originally obtained from LIS Database; presented in Caminada and Wang (2011); Leiden Budget Incidence Fiscal Redistribution Database.

LIS Keyfigs HH_Disp: Household Disposable Income, using the square root equivalence scale; LIS Inequality & Poverty Key Figures Database.

OECD HH_Before taxes, tr: Household Income before taxes and transfers; unnamed equivalence scale; OECD.StatExtracts database.

OECD HH_Disp: Household Disposable Income after taxes and transfers; unnamed equivalence scale; OECD.StatExtracts database.

SWIID HH_Market: Estimated Household Gross (pre-tax, pre-transfer) income; square root equivalence scale and Luxembourg Income Study data as the standard; Solt, Frederick, SWIID v4.0.

SWIID HH_Net: Estimated Household Disposable Income; square root equivalence scale and Luxembourg Income Study data as the standard; Solt, Frederick, SWIID v4.0.

USCB HH_Gross: Household Gross Monetary Income; no equivalence scale used; based on data from the Annual Social and Economic Supplement to the Census Bureau's Current Population Survey (CPS), United States Census Bureau (USCB).

WIID2 HH_Disp: Household Disposable Income; no equivalence scale used; originally from Brandolini (1998); based on data from the Current Population Survey (CPS), co-sponsored by the US Census Bureau and the US Bureau of Labor Statistics (BLS); values have a quality rating of "1"; United Nations University, WIDER-World Income Inequality Database (WIID2).

FURTHER READING

Books on Inequality by this Author

Inequality and Instability: A Study of the World Economy Just Before the Great Crisis. New York: Oxford University Press, 2012.

With Maureen Berner, ed., *Inequality and Industrial Change: A Global View*. New York: Cambridge University Press, 2001.

Created Unequal: The Crisis in American Pay. New York: The Free Press, 1998. A Twentieth Century Fund Book. Paperback edition, University of Chicago Press, 2000.

Articles on Inequality by this Author and with Co-authors from UTIP

"Unpacking the First Fundamental Law." *World Economic Review*, Issue No. 69 (October 2014). http://www.paecon.net/PAEReview/issue69/Galbraith69.pdf.

With Béatrice Halbach, Aleksandra Malinowska, Amin Shams, and Wenjie Zhang. "UTIP Global Inequality Data Sets 1963–2008: Updates, Revisions and Quality Checks." *UTIP Working Paper No. 68*, May 6, 2014.

With J. Travis Hale. "The Evolution of Economic Inequality in the United States, 1969–2012: Evidence from Data on Inter-industrial Earnings and Inter-regional Incomes." *World Economic Review* 3 (2013): 1–19. http://tinyurl.com/n2fbwst.

"Reducing Poverty: What Might We Learn?" *European Journal of Development Research* 0 (2011): 1–4. doi: 10.1057/ejdr.2011.22.

"Inequality and Economic and Political Change: A Comparative Perspective." *Cambridge Journal of Regions, Economy and Society* (2010): 1–15. doi: 10.1093/cjres/rsq014.

With Enrique Garcilazo. "Inequalities, Employment and Income Convergence in Europe: Evidence from Regional Data." In William Milberg and Pascal Petit, eds., *International Review of Applied Economics*, special issue on "Globalization, Growth and Economic Security: Varieties of Capitalism in the 21st Century," 24(3) (2010): 359–377. http://tinyurl.com/6couk88.

With Adem Y. Elveren. "Pay Inequality in Turkey in the Neoliberal Era." *European Journal of Comparative Economics* 6(2) (2009): 177–206.

With Sara Hsu and Wenjie Zhang. "Beijing Bubble, Beijing Bust: Inequality, Trade and Capital Flow into China." *Journal of Current Chinese Affairs/China Aktuell* 2 (2009): 3–26.

"Inequality, Unemployment and Growth: New Measures for Old Controversies." *Journal of Economic Inequality* 7(2) (2009): 189. http://www.springerlink.com/content/q601q00pq3280257/

With Travis Hale. "State Income Inequality and Presidential Election Turnout and Outcomes." *Social Science Quarterly* 89(4) (2008): 887–901. http://www3.interscience.wiley.com/journal/121455115/abstract?CRETRY=1&SRETRY=0.

With Travis Hale. "Salario y desigualdad de la renta en los E.E.U.U." *Claves de la Economía Mundial* (2008): 333–341.

With Laura Spagnolo and Daniel Munevar. "Inequidad salarial en Cuba durante el Período Especial." *América Latina Hoy* 48 (2008): 109–148.

With Corwin Priest and George Purcell. "Economic Equality and Victory in War: An Empirical Investigation." *Defense and Peace Economics* 18(5) (2007): 431–449.

"Global Inequality and Global Macroeconomics." *Journal of Policy Modeling* 29 (2007): 587–607. http://dx.doi.org/10.1016/j.jpolmod.2007.05.008.

With Laura Spagnolo and Sergio Pinto. "Economic Inequality and Political Power: A Comparative Analysis of Argentina and Brazil." *Business and Politics*, Berkeley Electronic Press, 9 (2007): 1.

With Travis Hale. "American Inequality: From IT Bust to Big Government Boom." *The Economists' Voice* 3(8) (2006): article 6.

With Enrique Garcilazo. "Pay Inequality in Europe 1995–2000: Convergence Between Countries and Stability Inside." *European Journal of Comparative Economics*, 2(2) (2005): 139–175.

With Hyunsub Kum. "Estimating the Inequality of Household Incomes: Toward a Dense and Consistent Global Data Set." *Review of Income and Wealth*, Series 51, Number 1 (March 2005): 115–143.

"Tracking the Rise of Inequality in Russia and China." *WIDER Angle* 2 (2005): 4–7.

"Global Inequality and Global Policy." *Journal of Catholic Social Thought* 2(1) (2005): 125–151.

With Deepshikha Roy Chowdhury and Sanjeev Shrivastava. "Pay Inequality in the Indian Manufacturing Sector, 1979–1998." *Economic and Political Weekly*, New Delhi, 39(28) (2004): 3139–3148.

With Ludmila Krytynskaia and Qifei Wang. "The Experience of Rising Inequality in Russia and China during the Transition." *European Journal of Comparative Economics* 1(1) (2004). Also in Russian in *Mir Peremen* (World of Transformations) 1(2) (2004): 87–100.

With Enrique Garcilazo. "Unemployment, Inequality and the Policy of Europe, 1984–2000." *Banca Nazionale del Lavoro Quarterly Review* LVII(228) (2004): 3–28. Reprinted in Richard P. F. Holt and Steven Pressman, eds., *Empirical Post Keynesian Economics: Looking at the Real World*. Armonk, NY: M. E. Sharpe, 2007, 44–69.

With Hyunsub Kum. "Inequality and Economic Growth: A Global View Based on Measures of Pay." *CESifo Economic Studies* 49(4) (2003): 527–556.

With Pedro Conceição. "Technological intensity and inter-sectoral dynamics of inequality: evidence from the OECD, 1970–1990." *International Journal of Technology Policy and Management* 2(3) (2002): 315–337.

"A Perfect Crime: Inequality in the Age of Globalization." *Daedalus* (Winter 2002): 11–25.

"The Importance of Being Sufficiently Equal." *Social Policy and Philosophy* 19(1) (2002). Also published in Ellen Frankel Paul, Fred D. Miller Jr., and Jeffrey Paul, eds. *Should Differences in Income and Wealth Matter?* New York: Cambridge University Press, 2002, 201–225.

With Pedro Conceição and Peter Bradford. "The Theil Index in Sequences of Nested and Hierarchical Grouping Structures: Implications for the Measurement of Inequality Through Time, with Data Aggregated at Different Levels of Industrial Classification." *Eastern Economic Journal* 27(4) (Fall 2001): 491–514.

"Inequality and Poverty." In *Vincentian Chair of Social Justice*, Vol. 5, 1999 Presentations (2000): 10–13.

With Pedro Filipe Teixeira da Conceição. "Constructing Long and Dense Time Series of Inequality Using the Theil Statistic." *Eastern Economic Journal* 26(1) (2000): 61–74.

With Paulo Du Pin Calmon, Pedro Filipe Teixeira da Conceição, Vidal Garza-Cantú and Abel Hibert. "The Evolution of Industrial Wage Inequality in Mexico and Brazil." *Review of Development Economics* 4(2) (2000): 194–203.

With Pedro Conceição and Pedro Ferreira. "Inequality and Unemployment in Europe: The American Cure." *New Left Review* 237 (September–October 1999): 28–51.

With Thomas Ferguson. "The American Wage Structure, 1920–1947." *Research in Economic History* 19 (1999): 205–257.

With Vidal Garza-Cantú. "Inequality in American Manufacturing Wages, 1920–1998: A Revised Estimate." *Journal of Economic Issues* 32 (Summer 1999): 735–743.

"Globalization and Pay." *Proceedings of the American Philosophical Society* 143(2) (1999): 178–186.

"Inequality and Unemployment: An Analysis across Time and Countries." *Research on Economic Inequality* 8 (1998). Daniel Slottje, Series editor, Stamford, CT: JAI Press, 121–154.

With Paulo Du Pin Calmon. "Wage Change and Trade Performance in U.S. Manufacturing Industries." *Cambridge Journal of Economics* 20(4) (1996): 433–450.

SELECTED BIBLIOGRAPHY

Aaberge, Rolf, Anders Björklund, Markus Jäntti, Mårten Palme, Peder Pedersen, Nina Smith, and Tom Wennemo. 1996. "Income Inequality and Income Mobility in the Scandinavian Countries Compared to the United States." *Working Paper Series in Economics and Finance 98,* Stockholm School of Economics, revised August 2002.

Atkinson, Anthony B., Thomas Piketty, and Emmanuel Saez. 2011. "Top Incomes in the Long Run of History." *Journal of Economic Literature,* American Economic Association, 49(1): 3–71.

Baker, Dean, Andrew Glyn, David Howell, and John Schmitt. 2002. "Labor Market Institutions and Unemployment: A Critical Assessment of the Cross-Country Evidence." *The Schwartz Center Working Paper No. 17.*

Birdsall, Nancy, David Ross, and Richard Sabot. 1995. "Inequality and Growth Reconsidered: Lessons from East Asia." *The World Bank Economic Review* 9(3): 477–508.

Black, William K. 2005. *The Best Way to Rob a Bank Is to Own One.* Austin: The University of Texas Press.

Bluestone, Barry, and Bennett Harrison. 1988. *The Great U-Turn: Corporate Restructuring and the Polarizing of America.* New York: Basic Books.

Bollen, Kenneth A. 1980. "Issues in the Comparative Measurement of Political Democracy." *American Sociological Review* 45(June): 370–390.

Bound, John, and George Johnson. 1992. "Changes in the Structure of Wages in the 1980s: An Evaluation of Alternative Explanations." *American Economic Review* 82: 371–392.

Brandolini, A. 1998. *A Bird's-Eye View of Long-Run Changes in Income Inequality.* Roma: Banca d'Italia Research Department.

Bremer, Stuart A. 1992. "Dangerous Dyads: Conditions Affecting the Likelihood of Interstate War, 1816–1965." *Journal of Conflict Resolution* 36(2): 309–341.

Calmon, Paulo Du Pin, Pedro Filipe Teixeira da Conceição, James K. Galbraith, Vidal Garza-Cantú, and Abel Hibert. 2000. "The Evolution of Industrial Wage Inequality in Mexico and Brazil." *Review of Development Economics* 4(2): 194–203.

Caminada, Koen, and Chen Wang. 2011. "Disentangling Income Inequality and the Redistributive Effect of Social Transfers and Taxes in 36 LIS Countries." Department of Economics Research Memorandum, Leiden Law School. http://www.law.leidenuniv.nl/org/fisceco/economie/hervormingsz/datawelfarestate.html.

Cobham, Alex. 2014. *Palma vs Gini: Measuring post-2015 inequality.* Center for Global Development, http://tinyurl.com/pkym9yo. Accessed December 19, 2014.

Conceição, Pedro, and James K. Galbraith. 2000. "Constructing Long and Dense Time Series of Inequality Using the Theil Statistic." *Eastern Economic Journal* 26(1): 61–74.

Conceição, Pedro, and James K. Galbraith. 2001. "Towards a New Kuznets Hypothesis: Theory and Evidence on Growth and Inequality." In *Inequality and Industrial Change: A Global View*, edited by James K. Galbraith and Maureen Berner. New York: Cambridge University Press.

Conceição, Pedro, James K. Galbraith, and Peter Bradford. 2001."The Theil Index in Sequences of Nested and Hierarchical Grouping Structures: Implications for the Measurement of Inequality Through Time, With Data Aggregated at Different Levels of Industrial Classification." *Eastern Economic Journal* 27(4): 491–514.

Conceição, Pedro, and Pedro Ferreira, 2000. *The Young Person's Guide to the Theil Index.* UTIP Working Paper No. 14, http://utip.gov.utexas.edu.

Darity, William A., Jr., and Samuel Myers. 1999. *Persistent Disparity: Race and Economic Inequality in the United States since 1945.* New York: Edward Elgar.

Deininger, Klaus, and Lyn Squire. 1996. "A New Data Set Measuring Income Inequality." *World Bank Economic Review*, World Bank Group, 10(3): 565–591.

Deininger, Klaus, and Lyn Squire. 1998. "New Ways of Looking at Old Issues: Inequality and Growth." *Journal of Development Economics* 57(2): 259–287.

DiNardo, John, and Jorn-Steffen Pischke. 1996. "The Returns to Computer Use Revisited: Have Pencils Changed the Wage Structure Too?" National Bureau of Economic Research Working Paper No. 5606, June.

Ferguson, Thomas, and James K. Galbraith. 1999. "The American Wage Structure, 1920–1947." *Research in Economic History* 19: 205–257.

Forbes, Kristin J. 2000. "A Reassessment of the Relationship between Inequality and Growth." *American Economic Review* 90(4): 869–887.

Galbraith, James K. 1998. *Created Unequal: The Crisis in American Pay.* New York: Free Press.

Galbraith, James K. 2008. *The Predator State: How Conservatives Abandoned the Free Market and Why Liberals Should Too.* New York: Free Press.

Galbraith, James K. 2012. *Inequality and Instability: A Study of the World Economy Just Before the Great Crisis.* New York: Oxford University Press.

Galbraith, James K. 2014. "Kapital for the 21st Century?" A Review of *Capital in the 21st Century,* by Thomas Piketty. *Dissent* (Spring): 77–82.

Galbraith, James K., Amin Shams, Béatrice Halbach, Aleksandra Malinowska, and Wenjie Zhang. 2014. "The UTIP Global Inequality Data Sets 1963–2008: Updates, Revisions and Quality Checks." *UTIP Working Paper No. 68.*

Galbraith, James K., and Enrique Garcilazo. 2004. "Unemployment, Inequality and the Policy of Europe: 1984–2000." *Banca Nazionale del Lavoro Quarterly Review* 57(228): 3–28.

Galbraith, James K., and George Purcell. 1999. "Inequality and State Violence: A Preliminary Report." *UTIP Working Paper No.4.* http://utip.gov.utexas.edu/papers/utip_04enc.pdf.

Galbraith, James K., and Hyunsub Kum. 2003. "Inequality and Economic Growth: A Global View Based on Measures of Pay." *CESifo Economic Studies* 49(4): 527–556.

Galbraith, James K., and Hyunsub Kum. 2005a. "Estimating the Inequality of Household Incomes: A Statistical Approach to the Creation of a Dense and Consistent Global Data Set." *Review of Income and Wealth* 1: 115–143.

Galbraith, James K., and Hyunsub Kum. 2005b. "Estimating the Inequality of Household Incomes: Toward a Dense and Consistent Global Data Set." *Review of Income and Wealth,* Series 51, No. 1 (March): 115–143.

Galbraith, James K., and J. Travis Hale. 2006. "American Inequality: From IT Bust to Big Government Boom." *The Economists' Voice* 3(8).

Galbraith, James K., Ludmila Krytynskaia, and Qifei Wang. 2004. "The Experience of Rising Inequality in Russia and China during the Transition." *The European Journal of Comparative Economics* 1(1): 87–106.

Galbraith, John Kenneth. 1958. *The Affluent Society.* Boston: Houghton-Mifflin.

Goldin, Claudia, and Lawrence Katz. 2010. *The Race Between Education and Technology.* Cambridge, MA: Belknap Press.

Gottschalk, Peter, and Timothy M. Smeeding. 1997. "Cross-National Comparisons of Earnings and Income Inequality." *Journal of Economic Literature* 35(2): 633–687.

Harris, John R., and Michael P. Todaro. 1970. "Migration, Unemployment and Development: A Two-Sector Analysis." *The American Economic Review* 60(1): 126–142.

Harrison, Mark. 1998. "The Economics of World War II: An Overview." In Mark Harrison, ed., *The Economics of World War II: Six Great Powers in International Comparison.* Cambridge: Cambridge University Press.

Heathcoat, Jonathan, Fabrizio Perri, and Giovanni L. Violante. 2010. "Unequal We Stand: An Empirical Analysis of Economic Inequality in the United States: 1967–2006." *Review of Economic Dynamics, Elsevier for the Society for Economic Dynamics* 13(1): 15–51.

Hirschleifer, Jack. 2001. *The Dark Side of Force: Economic Foundations of Conflict Theory.* New York: Cambridge University Press.

Howell, David. 1997. *Institutional Failure and the American Worker.* Rhinebeck, NY: Jerome Levy Economics Institute of Bard College Policy Brief.

Hsu, Sara. 2008. "The Effect of Political Regimes on Inequality, 1963–2008." *UTIP Working Paper No. 53.* http://utip.gov.utexas.edu/papers/utip_53.pdf.

"Income Distribution—Inequality." StatExtracts. Organisation for Economic Co-operation and Development (OECD). http://www oecd.org/els/soc/inequality-database.htm.

Kapstein, Ethan B. 2003. "Two Dismal Sciences Are Better Than One—Economics and the Study of National Security." *International Security* 27(3): 158–187.

Kennedy, Paul M. 1987. *The Rise and Fall of the Great Powers: Economic Change and Military Conflict from 1500 to 2000.* New York: Random House.

Keynes, John Maynard. 1919. *The Economic Consequences of the Peace.* London: MacMillan.

Kuznets, Simon. 1955. "Economic Growth and Income Inequality," Presidential Address to the American Economic Association, *American Economic Review*, 45 (1): 1–28. March.

Lawrence, Robert Z., and Matthew J. Slaughter. 1993. "International Trade and American Wages in the 1980's: Giant Sucking Sound or Small Hiccup?" *Brookings Papers on Economic Activity*, Fall 1993, No. 2.

Luxembourg Income Study. http://www.lisdatacenter.org/. Accessed December 19, 2014.

Luxembourg Income Study (LIS). 2005. Estimates calculated by WIDER using the unit record data provided in the LIS database as above in June 2005. Restricted online database.

Maoz, Zeev, and Nasrin Abdolah. 1989. "Regime Types and International Conflict, 1816–1976." *Journal of Conflict Resolution* 33 (March): 3–35.

Martin, Andrew. 1981. "Economic Stagnation and Social Stalemate in Sweden." In *Monetary Policy, Selective Credit Policy and Industrial Policy in France, Britain West Germany and Sweden*. Washington, DC: Joint Economic Committee.

Marx, Karl. 1867. *Capital*.

Mehta, Aashish, Jesus Felipe, Pilipinas Quising, and Shiela Camingue. 2013. "Where Have All the Educated Workers Gone? Services and Wage Inequalities in Three Asian Economies." *Metroeconomica* 64: 3; 6–497. doi: 10.1111/meca.12014.

Milanovic, Branko. 2012. *The Haves and the Have-Nots: A Brief and Idiosyncratic History of Global Inequality*. New York: Basic Books.

Mishel, Lawrence, and Natalie Sabadish. 2012. "How Executive Compensation and Financial-Sector Pay Have Fueled Income Inequality." *Economic Policy Institute Issue Brief #331*.

Olson, Mancur, and Richard Zeckhauser. 1966. "An Economic Theory of Alliances." *Review of Economics and Statistics* 48(3): 266–279.

Piketty, Thomas. 2014. *Capital in the Twenty-first Century*. Cambridge, MA: Harvard University Press.

Piketty, Thomas, et al. *The World Top Incomes Database*. http://topincomes.parisschoolofeconomics.eu/. Accessed December 19, 2014.

Procopius, History of the Wars, 7 vols., trans. H. B. Dewing. Cambridge, MA, and London: Harvard University Press and Wm. Heinemann, 1914; reprint ed., 1953–1954, II.11–23. Scanned and modernized by J. S. Arkenberg, Dept. of History, California State, Fullerton.

Rawls, John. 1971. *A Theory of Justice*. Cambridge, MA: Belknap Press of Harvard University Press.

Reiter, Dan, and Allan J. Stam. 2002. *Democracies at War*. Princeton, NJ: Princeton University Press.

Ricardo, David. 1817. *Principles of Political Economy and Taxation, and Notes on Malthus*, in Piero Sraffa, ed., 1951, *The Works and Correspondence of David Ricardo*. Cambridge: Cambridge University Press.

Rousseau, Jean-Jacques. 1755. *Discourse on the Origins of Inequality*.

Schumpeter, Joseph A. 1942. *Capitalism, Socialism and Democracy*. Cambridge, MA: Harvard University Press.

Small, Melvin, and J. David. Singer. 1976. "The War Proneness of Democratic Regimes, 1816–1965." *Jerusalem Journal of International Relations* 1(Summer): 50–69.

Small, Melvin, and J. David Singer. 1982. *Resort to Arms: International and Civil Wars 1816–1980*. Thousand Oaks, CA: Sage.

Smith, Adam. 1776. *An Inquiry into the Nature and Causes of the Wealth of Nations*.

Solt, Frederick. 2009. "Standardizing the World Income Inequality Database." *Social Science Quarterly* 90(2): 231–242.

Solt, Frederick. *The Standardized World Income Inequality Dataset*. http://myweb.uiowa.edu/fsolt/swiid/swiid.html. Accessed December 19, 2014.

Stiglitz, Joseph. 2014. *The Price of Inequality*. New York: W. W. Norton.

"The Distribution of Household Income and Federal Taxes, 2010." 2013. Report by the US Congressional Budget Office. Washington, DC. December.

Theil, Henri. 1972. *Statistical Decomposition Analysis: With Applications in the Social and Administrative Sciences*. Amsterdam-London: North Holland Publishing Company.

Tilly, Charles. 1998. *Durable Inequality*. Berkeley: University of California Press.

"Trends in the Distribution of Household Income Between 1979 and 2007." 2011. Report by the US Congressional Budget Office. Washington, DC. October.

US Census Bureau, Current Population Survey, Annual Social and Economic Supplements. Historical Income Table H-4. Washington, DC.

Van Zanden, J. L. 1995. "Tracing the Beginning of the Kuznets Curve: Western Europe during the Early Modern Period." *The Economic History Review* 48(4): 643–664.

Veblen, Thorstein. 1899. *Theory of the Leisure Class.*

Weede, Erich. 1984. "Democracy and War Involvement." *Journal of Conflict Resolution* 28(4): 649–664.

Weede, Erich. 1992. "Some Simple Calculations on Democracy and War Involvement." *Journal of Peace Research* 29(4): 377–383.

Wilkinson, Richard, and Kate Pickett. 2009. *The Spirit Level: Why More Equal Societies Almost Always Do Better.* London: Allan Lane.

Wolff, Edward N. 2010. "Recent Trends in Household Wealth in the United States: Rising Debt and the Middle-Class Squeeze—an Update to 2007." *Levy Institute Working Paper No. 589.* http://www.levyinstitute.org/pubs/wp_589.pdf. Accessed December 19, 2014.

Wood, Adrian. 1994. *North-South Trade, Employment and Inequality: Changing Fortunes in a Skill-Driven World.* Oxford: Clarendon Press.

World Bank. 2007. *World Development Indicators Online.* http://www.worldbank.org/.

World Income Inequality Database (WIID2). 2013. United Nations University—World Institute for Development Economics Research, UNU-WIDER.

Wright, Noah. "Data Visualization in *Capital in the 21st Century.*" *UTIP Working Paper No. 70.*

INDEX